Mastering Sublime Text

A concise guide to help you master the Sublime
Text skills, from basic setup through the art of theme
customization to the proficiency of plugin development

Dan Peleg

PUBLISHING

BIRMINGHAM - MUMBAI

Mastering Sublime Text

First published: December 2013

Production Reference: 1171213

Published by Packt Publishing Ltd.
Livery Place
35 Livery Street
Birmingham B3 2PB, UK.

ISBN 978-1-84969-842-9

www.packtpub.com

Cover Image by Gagandeep Sharma (er.gagansharma@gmail.com)

Credits

Author
Dan Peleg

Reviewers
James Brooks
Dougal Matthews
Matt Morrison
Jeffrey Sadeli

Acquisition Editors
Kevin Colaco
Llewellyn Rozario

Lead Technical Editor
Larissa Pinto

Technical Editors
Gauri Dasgupta
Monica John

Proofreader
Dan McMahon

Copy Editors
Roshni Banerjee
Tanvi Gaitonde
Mradula Hegde
Dipti Kapadia
Insiya Morbiwala
Deepa Nambiar
Alfida Paiva
Shambhavi Pai

Project Coordinator
Jomin Varghese

Indexer
Hemangini Bari

Production Coordinator
Nilesh Bambardekar

Cover Work
Nilesh Bambardekar

About the Author

Dan Peleg is an accomplished software engineer. As a former developer in the Israeli Intelligence Force, he holds extensive experience in both defense and robotic industries, and has previously lectured at DefCon conventions. Dan has developed unique algorithms for robotic platforms, specializes in a variety of software platforms, and currently works as the CTO for an American startup company.

I want to thank every plugin developer whose plugin is mentioned in this book. I would also like to thank Stuart Herbert for the content on PHPUnit, and Tom Lahat and Yali Saar for their support.

About the Reviewers

James Brooks has been programming for over a decade, starting out at the age of seven. He's worked his way through multiple languages from LOGO to C++ and back again. Having built a custom operating system and several half-baked games, he's now settled into web development. He is currently working at Blue Bay Travel.

Dougal Matthews is a Python developer based in Scotland. He works for Red Hat, where he helps out with OpenStack. Dougal is also involved in running a number of community events, groups, and conferences.

Matt Morrison, after trying every development environment available, discovered Sublime Text, and never looked back. He immediately fell in love with its emphasis on text-based configuration files, accessibility of Python API, and vibrant ecosystem of plugins and extensions contributed by the community. Being a tinkerer and a teacher at heart, Matt set about learning as much as he could about the software and sharing his knowledge and passion with others on StackOverflow, the Sublime forums, and elsewhere. He has authored two extensions on Package Control: the Neon Color Scheme, which aims to make as many languages look as good as possible; and Python Improved, a better Python language definition that fixes bugs in the original as well as introducing new features, including Django integration, IPython support in SublimeREPL, Python 3 function annotations, and more. He is also an active contributor of bug fixes and feature improvements for a number of other open source projects.

Despite his broad interests in all things computer-related, software development is only a (rather time-consuming) hobby. Matt received his Master's degree in Molecular Medicine from Penn State in 2005, and is employed as a scientist in his day job, working on cell and molecular biology. He is currently working in Biotech in the greater Boston area, and absolutely loves what he does. Matt has a blog about Sublime Text at `http://mattdmo.com`, and invites one and all to stop by and participate. You can find him on GitHub, StackOverflow, and Twitter as `MattDMo`.

> I would like to thank my wife Amy and my two little boys for their support and understanding.

Jeffrey Sadeli graduated from Rose-Hulman Institute of Technology in 2008 with a bachelor's degree in Computer Science. As a technology and design enthusiast, his passion lies in applying elegant technical solutions and beautiful designs to solve problems. Having worked for several years as a full-time software development engineer at Beckman Coulter developing automation applications, he is currently pursuing a master's degree in Business at Doshisha University.

www.PacktPub.com

Support files, eBooks, discount offers and more

You might want to visit www.PacktPub.com for support files and downloads related to your book.

Did you know that Packt offers eBook versions of every book published, with PDF and ePub files available? You can upgrade to the eBook version at www.PacktPub.com and as a print book customer, you are entitled to a discount on the eBook copy. Get in touch with us at service@packtpub.com for more details.

At www.PacktPub.com, you can also read a collection of free technical articles, sign up for a range of free newsletters and receive exclusive discounts and offers on Packt books and eBooks.

http://PacktLib.PacktPub.com

Do you need instant solutions to your IT questions? PacktLib is Packt's online digital book library. Here, you can access, read and search across Packt's entire library of books.

Why Subscribe?

- Fully searchable across every book published by Packt
- Copy and paste, print and bookmark content
- On demand and accessible via web browser

Free Access for Packt account holders

If you have an account with Packt at www.PacktPub.com, you can use this to access PacktLib today and view nine entirely free books. Simply use your login credentials for immediate access.

Table of Contents

Preface

Mastering Sublime Text will put you at the frontier of modern software development. It will teach you how to leverage Sublime for anything from mobile games to missile protection. Above all, this book will help you harness the power of other Sublime users and always stay on top in this ever-changing world. The book takes you from the early stages of navigating through the platform and moves on by teaching you how to fully customize your installation, test, debug, and eventually create and share your own plugins to help take this community forward.

What this book covers

Chapter 1, Installing Sublime Text, helps you get started on different platforms and with basic settings.

Chapter 2, Code Editing, covers navigation techniques, shortcuts, and must-have plugins.

Chapter 3, Snippets, Macros, and Key Bindings, covers snippets usage, macros, and key binding management.

Chapter 4, Customization and Theme Development, explains how to customize your workspace, from colors to split screens.

Chapter 5, Unravelling Vintage Mode, explains what Vintage Mode is, how to set it up, and how to take advantage of it.

Chapter 6, Testing Using Sublime, explains how to test your code in several different languages.

Chapter 7, Debugging Using Sublime, explains how to use Sublime Text for debugging your code in different languages.

Chapter 8, Developing Your Own Plugin, will guide you through developing your own Sublime Text plugins and publishing them to the community.

What you need for this book

You will require an Internet connection and Git installed on your system; the rest will be specified in each chapter.

Who this book is for

This book is for developers in any type of programming language who want to start using Sublime Text or perfect their existing skills, regardless of whether they are evaluating it for free or using a licensed version. No knowledge of Sublime Text or any other code editor or IDE is required.

Conventions

In this book, you will find a number of styles of text that distinguish between different kinds of information. Here are some examples of these styles, and an explanation of their meaning.

Code words in text are shown as follows: "This will reload your `.bash_profile` with the newly added directory."

A block of code is set as follows:

```
{
    "font_size": 14,
    "always_show_minimap_viewport": true,
    "ignored_packages":
    [
        "Vintage"
    ]
}
```

Any command-line input or output is written as follows:

```
sudo ln -s /opt/sublime_text_3/sublime_text /usr/bin/subl
```

New terms and **important words** are shown in bold. Words that you see on the screen, in menus or dialog boxes for example, appear in the text like this: "I recommend adding Sublime to the explorer context by ticking **Add to explorer context menu**."

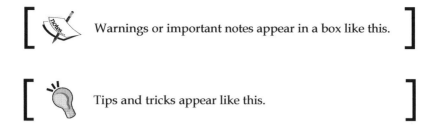

Warnings or important notes appear in a box like this.

Tips and tricks appear like this.

Reader feedback

Feedback from our readers is always welcome. Let us know what you think about this book—what you liked or may have disliked. Reader feedback is important for us to develop titles that you really get the most out of.

To send us general feedback, simply send an e-mail to feedback@packtpub.com, and mention the book title via the subject of your message.

If there is a topic that you have expertise in and you are interested in either writing or contributing to a book, see our author guide on www.packtpub.com/authors.

Customer support

Now that you are the proud owner of a Packt book, we have a number of things to help you to get the most from your purchase.

Errata

Although we have taken every care to ensure the accuracy of our content, mistakes do happen. If you find a mistake in one of our books—maybe a mistake in the text or the code—we would be grateful if you would report this to us. By doing so, you can save other readers from frustration and help us improve subsequent versions of this book. If you find any errata, please report them by visiting http://www.packtpub.com/submit-errata, selecting your book, clicking on the **errata submission form** link, and entering the details of your errata. Once your errata are verified, your submission will be accepted and the errata will be uploaded on our website, or added to any list of existing errata, under the Errata section of that title. Any existing errata can be viewed by selecting your title from http://www.packtpub.com/support.

Piracy

Piracy of copyright material on the Internet is an ongoing problem across all media. At Packt, we take the protection of our copyright and licenses very seriously. If you come across any illegal copies of our works, in any form, on the Internet, please provide us with the location address or website name immediately so that we can pursue a remedy.

Please contact us at copyright@packtpub.com with a link to the suspected pirated material.

We appreciate your help in protecting our authors, and our ability to bring you valuable content.

Questions

You can contact us at questions@packtpub.com if you are having a problem with any aspect of the book, and we will do our best to address it.

1
Installing Sublime Text

This chapter will guide us through installing Sublime Text on all the supported platforms. We will also cover advanced installation and basic navigation around Sublime. This chapter is aimed at new users, but we recommend you flip through it even if you are already familiar with Sublime Text.

In this chapter, we will cover the following topics:

- Installing Sublime Text on OS X
- Installing Sublime Text on Windows 32/64 bit
- Installing Sublime Text on Linux 32/64 bit
- Getting to know the Data and Packages directories
- Running Sublime for the first time
- Installing the Package Control ASAP

Preparing for Sublime Text Installation

This chapter serves as a quick installation reference for users who are new to Sublime Text, and covers all supported operating systems. We will also cover advanced installation techniques such as adding Sublime to our **Command Line Interface (CLI)** and to Ubuntu's action bar. Please refer to the appropriate section depending on your operating system.

 At the time of writing this book, Sublime Text 3 was in Beta. Follow #sublimehq on Twitter for version updates.

Installing Sublime Text on OS X

This section will explain how to install Sublime Text on OS X 10.7 or later, as required.

First go to http://www.sublimetext.com/3 and click on the download link for OS X. A file called Sublime Text Build #.dmg will be downloaded. Open this file and we will see the following window:

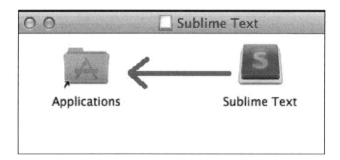

Simply drag the **Sublime Text** icon into the **Applications** folder and wait for the application to be copied.

We have just installed Sublime on our OS X! Is that all? No, we can also get the bleeding edge version from here: http://www.sublimetext.com/3dev. Bleeding edge versions are available for registered users only and are more susceptible to bugs.

Working with Sublime CLI

Sublime Text ships with a CLI called subl, but this CLI isn't added to our environment by default. We want to be able to use it straight from our terminal, so we need to add a symbolic link called **subl** to the subl executable.

```
ln -s /Applications/Sublime\ Text.app/Contents/SharedSupport/bin/subl
/usr/local/bin/subl
```

To see if it worked, type subl filename in the terminal where filename is the file you want to edit. Did it work? If not, then we need to add our folder that contains the new symlink to the environment. Run the following command:

```
open ~/.bash_profile
```

The first line of the file should start with export PATH=. It contains all the directories that will be looked into for executable binaries when we type a command in the terminal. Since we created a symlink to subl inside the /usr/local/bin directory, we will add it to the path by adding it to the directories:

```
export PATH=/usr/local/bin[...]
```

[...] represents other directories that would be listed on the same line, separated by a colon.

Now, run the following code before continuing:

```
source ~/.bash_profile
```

This will reload your `.bash_profile` with the newly added directory.

Sublime CLI should work now; try one of the following commands:

```
subl filename ("filename" is the filename to edit)
subl foldername ("foldername" is the folder to open)
subl . (to open the current directory)
```

That's it! We have Sublime Text with CLI running on our OS X!

Installing Sublime Text on Windows 32/64 bit

This section will explain how to install Sublime Text on Windows 7/8, 32/64 bit. It is important to get the right version because the 64-bit version won't run on a 32-bit PC.

Go to `http://www.sublimetext.com/3` and download the relevant file for 32-bit or 64-bit. A file called `Sublime Text Build # Setup.exe` will be downloaded. Open the file and you will be guided through the setup. Click on **Next** and choose setup location. Next, add Sublime to the explorer context by American English: should use "checking" **Add to explorer context menu** as shown in the following screenshot:

Select Additional Tasks
Which additional tasks should be performed?

Select the additional tasks you would like Setup to perform while installing Sublime Text 3, then click Next.

☑ Add to explorer context menu

Then, finish the installation. We have just installed Sublime! Are we done? Not yet.

Adding Sublime to the environment

We want to add Sublime to our environment so we can use it straight from the command line. Open **Run** by pressing *WinKey + R* and enter `sysdm.cpl`, as shown in the following screenshot:

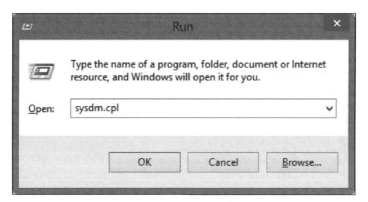

Click on **OK**, the System Properties window should open. Now, go to the **Advanced** tab and click on the **Environment Variables...** button at the bottom-right corner. Environment variables should open, look for the **Path** variable in **System variables**, double-click it to open the **Edit System Variable** window, and add your Sublime installation path to the end of the **Variable value** field prefixed with a semicolon, as shown in the following screenshot:

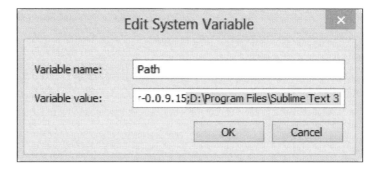

As we can see, my installation path is `D:\Program Files\Sublime Text 3`. Click on **OK**. Now we can run Sublime from the command line by typing `sublime_text filename` where `filename` is the file to edit. But the `sublime_text` command is too long to type every time we want to open a file with Sublime. Go to your installation directory and create a new file named `subl.bat`. Paste the following code into the file:

```
@echo off
start sublime_text.exe %*
```

The first line turns off the echo of the .bat file. This means that we won't see any output when we run the file. The second line will start the sublime_text executable with the given parameters.

Save the .bat file and open a new command line. We can now use the following commands in our command line:

```
subl filename ("filename" is the filename to edit)
```

```
subl foldername ("foldername" is the folder to open)
```

```
subl . (to open the current directory)
```

That's it; we have Sublime on our Windows PC!

Installing Sublime Text on Linux

This section will explain how to install Sublime Text on different Linux distributions.

Installing Sublime Text on Ubuntu 32/64 bit

This section will explain how to install Sublime Text on Ubuntu 32/64 bit.

There are a few different options for installing Sublime Text on your Ubuntu; we will use the **Personal Package Archive (PPA)** one. For this, we need to add the PPA that contains the Sublime Package. PPA is a software repository that contains packages that can be installed by Ubuntu's Launchpad.

To add the repository, run the following from the terminal:

```
sudo add-apt-repository ppa:webupd8team/sublime-text-3
```

```
sudo apt-get update
```

```
sudo apt-get install sublime-text-installer
```

To install Sublime Text 3 on our Ubuntu, we can now use the following commands:

```
subl filename ("filename" is the filename to edit)
```

```
subl foldername ("foldername" is the folder to open)
```

```
subl . (to open the current directory)
```

We can also see the **Sublime** icon on Ubuntu's action bar, which is typically on the left-hand side, as shown in the following screenshot:

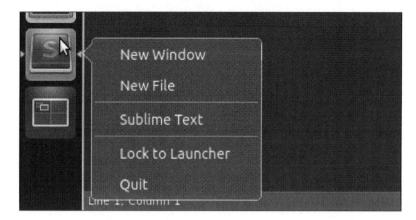

Setting Sublime Text as the default editor

After we have installed Sublime, we want to set it as the default editor for everything! To do that, simply open the `defaults.list` file of Ubuntu by using the following command:

```
sudo subl /usr/share/applications/defaults.list
```

And replace all occurrences of `gedit.desktop` with `sublime-text.desktop`.

Installing Sublime Text on other Linux distributions

Installing Sublime on a Linux other than Ubuntu takes a little longer, but we will do it as fast as possible! We start by going to `http://www.sublimetext.com/3` and downloading the desired tarball for 32-bit or 64-bit.

 Notice that we do not download the Ubuntu one but the tarball.

After downloading, let's open our terminal and navigate to the **Downloads** folder:

```
cd ~/Downloads
```

The downloaded file is compressed using TAR. We will have to NTAR it first by running the following command:

```
tar xf sublime_text_3_build_3047_x64.tar.bz2
```

 Your filename might be different depending on your build and architecture.

Move the extracted folder to /op:

```
sudo mv sublime_text_3 /opt/
```

We want to make a symbolic link so that we can run Sublime straight from the terminal:

```
sudo ln -s /opt/sublime_text_3/sublime_text /usr/bin/subl
```

Now, we have Sublime installed and can use the following commands to open the directory:

```
subl filename ("filename" is the filename to edit)
subl foldername ("foldername" is the folder to open)
subl . (to open the current directory)
```

Adding a desktop file

Some distributions such as OpenSUSE, Ubuntu, or GNOME, use .desktop files. These files are for the desktop/action bar launch icons.

Let's add Sublime's .desktop file to the environment. It's good for us that Sublime comes with the file already and we don't need to write it. Just copy the file to the right location using the following command:

```
sudo cp /opt/sublime_text/sublime_text.desktop /usr/share/applications/
```

Your distribution may not provide /usr/share/applications, in which case you'll have to copy the file to ~/.local/share/applications.

Getting to know the Data and Packages directories

After the successful installation of Sublime on our system, we can begin to understand what was actually being installed and how can we take advantage of it.

In this section I will use Windows shortcuts. So when I use *Ctrl+?*, it will be the same as using *Command+?* on a Mac.

The Data directory

From the official Sublime docs:

> *Nearly all of the interesting files for users live under the Data directory.*

The location of the Data directory is platform-dependent:

- **Windows**: `%APPDATA%\Sublime Text 3`
- **OS X**: `~/Library/Application Support/Sublime Text 3`
- **Linux**: `~/.config/sublime-text-3`

We should see at least three directories inside the Data directory:

- **Installed Packages**: This contains a copy of every `sublime-package` installed. It's used to restore packages.
- **Local**: This stores all the information about our current and previous session. This is used to restore Sublime to the stage we were in, when we last quit Sublime.
- **Packages**: This contains all package folders that Sublime will load.

The Packages directory

The following is written on the official Sublime docs:

> "*This is a key directory*"

This directory contains all the resources for supported programming, markup languages, and custom plugins. We will refer to this folder as `Packages`.

We can also access the Packages directory from Sublime's main menu by navigating to **Preferences** | **Browse Packages...** on Windows or Linux, and by navigating to **Sublime Text** | **Preferences** | **Browse Packages...** on OS X.

The User package

This package is present at Packages/User and contains all custom plugins, snippets, macros, and user preferences. Let's make our first tweak!

Open Packages/User/Preferences.sublime-settings. We should see the following code:

```
{
    "font_size": 14,
    "ignored_packages":
    [
        "Vintage"
    ]
}
```

Try changing the font size and click on **Save** or *Ctrl + S*. Our font size has changed! We can also achieve this effect by pressing *Ctrl + -* to decrease the font size and *Ctrl + +* to increase the font size. In Linux or Windows, this can also be achieved by holding the *Ctrl* key while zooming in and out.

Delving into packages, plugins, snippets, and macros

Almost every corner and pixel of Sublime Text can be tweaked, extended, or customized. All this customization is based on JSON, XML, Python, and Sublime files. A package is basically a folder that contains all resources that belong together, and it gives Sublime a new functionality or customization. This is all we need to know for now.

Running Sublime for the first time

Open a random code project. We can do it by typing the following command:

```
subl projectfolder
```

In the preceding command, `projectfolder` is the path of the folder we wish to open. We can also open an empty Sublime window and drag the desired folder into it. The Sublime window is shown in the following screenshot:

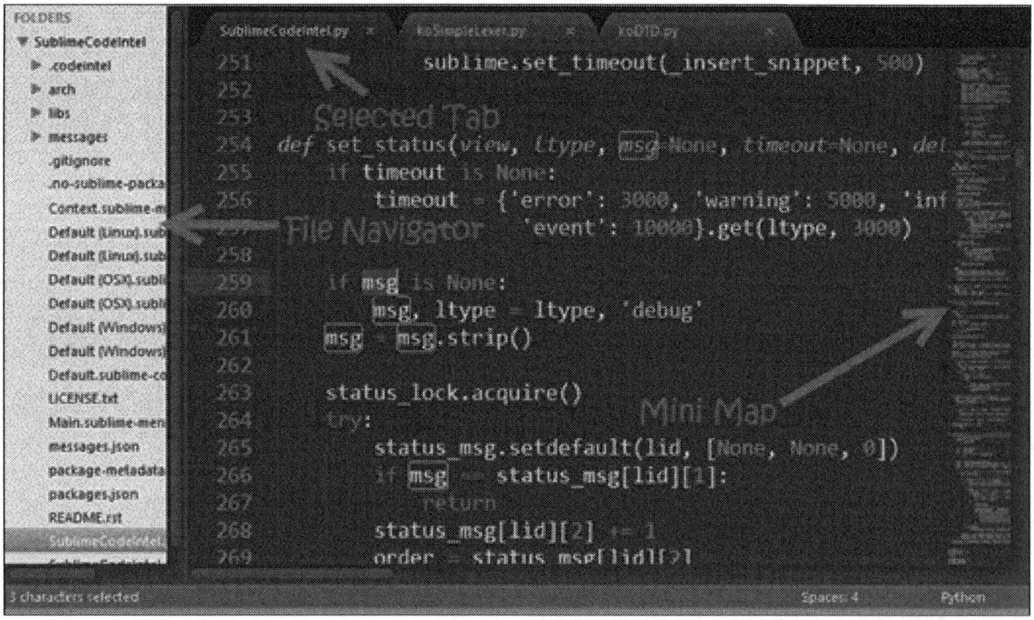

![Sublime Text window screenshot showing File Navigator, Selected Tab, and Mini Map]

In the preceding screenshot, on the left-hand side we can see the File Navigator side bar that contains all the open folders in a hierarchy. At the top, we can see the tabs that are currently open, with the selected one highlighted. On the right-hand side, we can see the **Mini Map**. In Sublime 3, the Mini Map viewport that indicates the current position in the file has been removed. Let's bring it back!

Press *Ctrl + O* and open the user preferences, or go to **Preferences | Settings-User**. As you probably noticed, the file is written in the JSON format.

> If you are not familiar with JSON, please go to http:// en.wikipedia.org/wiki/JSON#Data_types.2C_syntax_and_ example or http://JSON.org.

We need to add the following key value to the file:

```
"always_show_minimap_viewport": true,
```

Press *Ctrl + S* to save. Our file should now look like the following:

```
{
    "font_size": 14,
    "always_show_minimap_viewport": true,
    "ignored_packages":
    [
        "Vintage"
    ]
}
```

Because Sublime parses things as soon as they get saved, we should be able to see the Mini Map viewport immediately!

Simple navigation

Let's go back to our file using **Goto Anything** (shown in the following screenshot), one of Sublime's best features, by pressing *Ctrl + P*:

We can even highlight the Mini Map by setting `"draw_minimap_border": true` in our settings file.

As you can see, the **Go To** window opens after indexing all files that are on the side bar. We can navigate by typing the file name, acronyms, extension, or prefix.

This search feature is called **Fuzzy Text Search** or **Approximate string matching**.

Press *Esc* to close the **Go To** window. We are going to use this a lot while developing a large project, so we should feel comfortable with it before moving on.

Try closing the current tab by pressing *Ctrl + W*. Now if no tab is left open, you can open a new one by pressing *Ctrl + N*, or even open a new window by pressing *Ctrl + Shift + N*.

 If you press *Ctrl + W* on Windows or Linux when no tabs are open, the window itself will close.

To jump between open tabs in Windows or Linux, simply press *Alt + #* (where # is the sequential number of the tab from left to right), or press *Command + #* for OS X. In Windows or Linux, we can also go to the **Next** or **Previous** tab by pressing *Ctrl + PageUp* and *Ctrl + PageDown* respectively. The same can be done by pressing *Option + Command + →* or *Option + Command + ←* in OS X. Another nice navigation feature is the tab stack. To go forward in the stack, press *Ctrl + Tab*, and press *Ctrl + Shift + Tab* to go backwards. On OS X also, it's *Control* and not *Command* this time.

There are more nice Go To features such as `Go To line` by pressing *Ctrl + G*, and `Go To matching bracket` with *Ctrl + M*.

Sublime's command palette

One of the most important features is the command palette where all the custom features or plugins can be accessed. Open the command palette by pressing *Ctrl + Shift + P*, or *Command + Shift + P* on OS X. We should see the following screenshot:

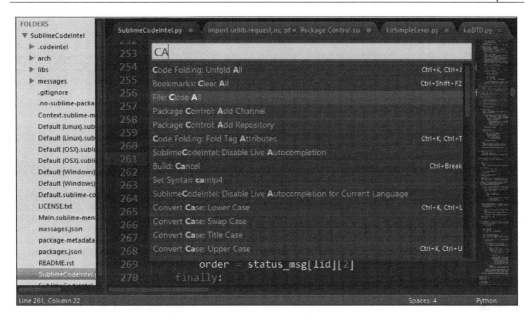

This window is using the same search algorithm that the **Go To Anything** window uses. We can see that I typed **CA** and I get the **Close All** command. Pressing *Enter* will close all open tabs. Don't worry, it will notify if a file we are trying to close has not been saved. We can see any keyboard shortcuts to the right of each command.

The Python console

Sublime comes with an embedded Python interpreter. It's a useful tool to inspect the editor's settings, quickly test API calls while developing plugins, or just do simple math. To open the Python console, press *Ctrl+`* or go to **View | Show Console** from the main menu. The following screenshot shows a Python console:

```
writing file /C/Users/Danpe/AppData/Roaming/Sublime Text 3/Packages/User/
Preferences.sublime-settings with encoding UTF-8 (atomic)
reloading Packages/User/Preferences.sublime-settings
found 1 files for base name Default.sublime-theme
theme loaded
>>> 1+1
2
```

Line 5, Column 17   Spaces: 4   Plain Text

It's important to know that Sublime comes with its own Python interpreter on Windows and Linux, and it's separate from your system's Python installation. Modifying your system's version of python, such as replacing it with the MacPorts version, can cause problems with Sublime Text.

Installing the Package Control ASAP

We learned that Sublime has Packages that help us customize our Sublime experience. But how can we find the packages that suit our needs? And how do we install different packages? That's why we have Package Control `https://sublime.wbond.net/` The Package Control is a non-official open source plugin that lets us navigate through thousands of mainly open source packages ready to install! There are some closed source (commercial) plugins available, such as **Sublimemerge** and **SFTP**.

Let's start by installing the `Package Control` plugin into Sublime. We do it by opening the console *Ctrl +* ` and copying the following code:

```
import urllib.request,os; pf = 'Package Control.sublime-package';
ipp = sublime.installed_packages_path(); urllib.request.install_
opener( urllib.request.build_opener( urllib.request.ProxyHandler()
) ); open(os.path.join(ipp, pf), 'wb').write(urllib.request.urlopen(
'http://sublime.wbond.net/' + pf.replace(' ','%20')).read())
```

 If you are having trouble installing the Package Control ASAP using the preceding code, please visit `http://sublime.wbond.net/ installation`.

This code will download the `Package Control` package and place it inside the `Installed Packages` directory. After it has finished installing, open the command palette and navigate to **Package Control | Install Package**. Then press *Enter* and you will notice **Loading repositories [=]** in the status bar.

Line 18, Column 27; Loading repositories [=]   Spaces: 4   Plain Text

After it finishes loading, a new window will open with all the packages available for instant installation!

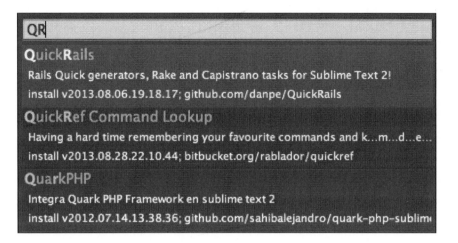

What we see in this screenshot is the package title, description, version, and the repository link. To install, simply press *Enter* and the new installed features will appear in the command palette.

Summary

By the end of this chapter we should have Sublime Text with Package Control installed on our system, and all the necessary shortcuts for Sublime commands in the CLI. We have also learned how to navigate the user interface and had a sneak peak of some of the cool features of Sublime.

In the next chapter, we are going to touch some code and learn more advanced techniques for navigating and code editing in Sublime.

2
Code Editing

This chapter will guide us from Sublime's basic features to its most advanced ones, and explore techniques to use while editing code. We will also install two important plugins for most languages and master Sublime's Shortcuts Map.

In this chapter we will cover the following topics:

- Discovering Search and Replace
- Mastering Column and Multiple Selection
- Navigating through Project, Files, and Classes
- Using the must-have SublimeCodeIntel
- Linting with SublimeLinter
- The must-know Shortcuts Map

Discovering Search and Replace

Search and Replace is one of the common actions for any text editor. Sublime Text has two main search features:

- Single file
- Multiple files

Before covering these topics, let's talk about the best tool available for searching text and especially, patterns; namely, Regular Expressions.

Regular Expressions

Regular Expressions can find complex patterns in text. To take full advantage of the Search and Replace features of Sublime, you should at least know the basics of Regular Expressions, also known as regex or regexp. Regular Expressions can be really annoying, painful, and joyful at the same time!

We won't cover Regular Expressions in this book because it's an endless topic. We will only note that Sublime Text uses the Boost's Perl Syntax for Regular Expressions; this can be found at `http://www.boost.org/doc/libs/1_47_0/ libs/regex/doc/html/boost_regex/syntax/perl_syntax.html`

I recommend going to `http://www.regular-expressions.info/ quickstart.html` if you are not familiar with Regular Expressions.

Search and Replace – a single file

Let's open the Search panel by pressing *Ctrl + F* on Windows and Linux or *command + F* on OS X. The search panel options can be controlled using keyboard shortcuts:

Search panel options	Windows/Linux	OS X
Toggle Regular Expressions	*Alt + R*	*command + Option + R*
Toggle Case Sensitivity	*Alt + C*	*command + Option + C*
Toggle Exact Match	*Alt + W*	*command + Option + W*
Find Next	*Enter*	*Enter*
Find Previous	*Shift + Enter*	*Shift + Enter*
Find All	*Alt + Enter*	*Option + Enter*

As we can see in the following screenshot, we have the **Regular Expression** option turned on:

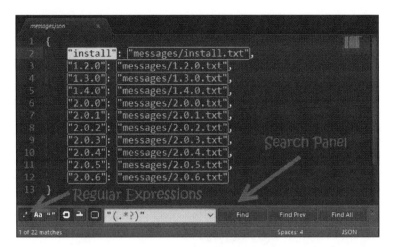

Let's try Search and Replace now by pressing *Ctrl + H* on Windows and Linux or *Option + command + F* on OS X and examining the following screenshot:

We can see that this time, both the Regular Expression option and the Case Sensitivity option are turned on. Because of the Case Sensitivity option being on, line **8** isn't selected, the pattern `messages/(\d)` doesn't match line **2** because `\d` only matches numbers, and the `\1` on the **Replace with** field will replace match group number `1`, indicated by the parentheses around `\d`.

 We can also refer to the group by using `$1` instead of `\1`.

Let's see what happens after we press *Ctrl* + *Alt* + *Enter* for **Replace All**:

```
messages.json

1  {
2      "install": "messages/install.txt",
3      "1.2.0": "message/1.2.0.txt",
4      "1.3.0": "message/1.3.0.txt",
5      "1.4.0": "message/1.4.0.txt",
6      "2.0.0": "message/2.0.0.txt",
7      "2.0.1": "message/2.0.1.txt",        After Replace
8      "2.0.2": "Messages/2.0.2.txt",
9      "2.0.3": "message/2.0.3.txt",
10     "2.0.4": "message/2.0.4.txt",
11     "2.0.5": "message/2.0.5.txt",
12     "2.0.6": "message/2.0.6.txt"
13 }
9 characters selected: Made 9 replacements          Spaces: 4      JSON
```

We can see that lines **2** and **8** still say `messages` and not `message`; that's exactly what we expected!

The incremental search

Incremental search is another cool feature that is here to save us keyboard clicks. We can bring up the incremental search panel by pressing *Ctrl* + *I* on Windows and Linux or *command* + *I* on OS X. The only difference between the incremental search and a regular search is the behavior of the *Enter* key; in incremental searches, the *Enter* key will select the next match and dismiss the search panel. This saves us from pressing *Esc* to dismiss the regular search panel.

Search and Replace – multiple files

Sublime Text also allows a multiple file search by pressing *Ctrl + Shift + F* or *command + Shift + F* on OS X. The same shortcuts from the single file search also apply here; the difference is that we have the **Where** field and a **...** button near it. The `Where` field determines where the files can be searched for; we can define the scope of the search in several ways:

- Adding individual directories (Unix-style paths, even on Windows)
- Adding/excluding files based on the wildcard pattern
- Adding Sublime-symbolic locations such as `<open folders>`, `<open files>`

We can also combine filters by separating them with commas in the following manner:

```
/C/Users/Dan/Cool Project,*.rb,<open files>
```

This will look in all files in `C:\Users\Dan\Cool Project` that end with `.rb` and are currently open by Sublime.

Results will be opened in a new tab called **Find Results,** containing all found results separated by file paths. Double clicking on a result will take you to the exact location of the result in the original file.

Mastering Column and Multiple Selection

Multiple Selections is one of Sublime's coolest features; TextMate users might be familiar with it. So how can we select multiple lines? We select one line like we usually do and select the second line while holding *Ctrl* or *command* on OS X. We can also subtract a line by holding the *Alt* key or *command + Shift* keys on OS X. This feature is really useful and it is recommended that you play with it. The following are some shortcuts that can help us feel more comfortable with multiple selections:

Multiple selection action	Windows/Linux	OS X
Return to Single Selection Mode	*Esc*	*Esc*
Undo last selection motion	*Ctrl + U*	*command + U*
Add next occurrence of selected text to selection	*Ctrl + D*	*command + D*
Add all occurrences of selected text to selection	*Alt + F3*	*Control + command + G*
Turn Single Linear Selection into Block Selection	*Ctrl + Shift + L*	*Shift + command + L*

Column Selection

The Column Selection feature is one of my favorites! We can select multiple lines by pressing *Shift* and dragging the right mouse button on Windows and Linux, or Linux and pressing *Option* and dragging the left mouse button on OS X. Here we want to remove the letter **s** from **messages**, as shown in the following screenshot:

We have selected all s using Column selection; now we just need to hit backspace to delete them.

Navigating through everything

Sublime is known for its ability to quickly move between and around files and lines. In this section, we are going to master how to navigate our code quickly and easily.

Go To Anything

We already learned how to use the **Go To Anything** feature, but it can do more than just searching for filenames. We can conduct a fuzzy search inside a "fuzzily found" file. Really? Yeah, we can. For example, we can type the following inside the Go To Anything window:

```
isl#wld
```

This will make Sublime perform a fuzzy search for wld inside the file that we found by fuzzy searching isl; it can thus find the word **world** inside a file named **island**.

We can also perform a fuzzy search in the current file by pressing *Ctrl +;* **in Windows or Linux and** *command* + *P,* # in OS X. It is very common to use fuzzy search inside HTML files because it immediately shows all the elements and classes that match, accelerating navigation.

Symbol search

Sometimes we want to search for a specific function or class inside the current file. With Sublime we can do it simply by pressing *Ctrl* + *R* on Windows or Linux and *command* + *R* on OS X.

Projects

A project is a group of files and folders. To save a project we just need to add folders and files to the sidebar, and then from the menu, we navigate to **Project | Save Project As…**

The saved file is our projects data, and it is stored in a JSON formatted file with a `.sublime-project` extension. The following is a sample project file:

```json
{
    "folders":
    [
        {
            "path": "src",
            "follow_symlinks": true
        },
        {
            "path": "docs",
            "name": "Documentation",
            "file_exclude_patterns": ["*.xml"]
        }
    ],
```

```
"settings":
{
    "tab_size": 6
},
"build_systems":
[
    {
        "name": "List",
        "shell_cmd": "ls -l"
    }
]
}
```

As we can see in the preceding code, there are three elements written as JSON arrays.

Folders

Each folder must have a valid folder path that can be absolute or relative to the project directory, which is where the project file is. A folder can also include the following keys:

- name: This is the name that will be shown on the sidebar
- file_execlude_pattern: This folder will exclude all the files matching the given Regular Expression
- file_include_pattern: This folder will include only files matching the given Regular Expression
- folder_execlude_pattern: This folder will exclude all subfolders matching the given Regular Expression
- folder_include_pattern: This folder will include only subfolders matching the given Regular Expression
- follow_symlinks: This will include symlinks if set to true

Settings

The project-specific settings array will contain all the settings that we want to apply only to this project. These settings will override our global user settings.

Build systems

In an array of build system definitions, we must specify a name for each definition; these build systems will then be specified in **Tools | Build Systems**.

 For more information about build systems, please visit http://sublimetext.info/docs/en/reference/build_systems.html.

Navigating between projects

To switch between projects quickly, we can press *Ctrl + Alt + P* in Windows or Linux and *Control + command + P* in OS X.

Using the must-have SublimeCodeIntel

SublimeCodeIntel is a must-have plugin. Its main features are:

- The Jump to Symbol Definition feature, which allows a user to jump to the file and line of the defining symbol

- It Imports autocomplete and displays the available modules/symbols in real time

- The Function Call tooltips display information in the status bar about the working function

Installing SublimeCodeIntel

We can easily install this plugin using the Package Control utility that we installed earlier. Let's open it up by pressing *Ctrl + Shift + P* in Windows or Linux and *command + Shift + P* in OS X. Choose **Install Package** and install the **SublimeCodeIntel** plugin. We will then need to restart Sublime.

When it first starts, SublimeCodeIntel needs to build an index of the languages you're using. Depending on the number of modules/libraries you have installed and the size and complexity of the project you're working on, this can take some time. Be patient though, it will be well worth it when it's ready.

Using SublimeCodeIntel

After SublimeCodeIntel finishes indexing, start typing code as usual; autocomplete will pop up whenever it's available. SublimeCodeIntel shortcuts map:

SublimeCodeIntel action	Windows	Linux	OS X
Jump to definition	*Alt + Left Mouse Click*	*Super + Left Mouse Click*	*Control + Left Mouse Click*
Jump to definition	*Control + Windows + Alt + Up*	*Control + Super + Alt + Up*	*Control + command + Option + Up*
Go Back	*Control + Windows + Alt + Left*	*Control + Super + Alt + Left*	*Control + command + Option + Left*
Manual Code Intelligence	*Control + Shift + Space*	*Control + Shift + Space*	*Control + Shift + Space*

Configuring SublimeCodeIntel

To add additional libraries such as Django, extra paths for Python or extra paths to look for `.js` files for JavaScript, we can edit the `codeintel` config file that is located at `~/.codeintel/config` in Linux or OS X and `C:\Users\username\.codeintel\config` in Windows. By default, this file will be an empty JSON-formatted file. Here is an example for optional configuration:

```
{
    "PHP": {
        "php": '/usr/bin/php',
        "phpExtraPaths": [],
        "phpConfigFile": 'php.ini'
    },
    "JavaScript": {
        "javascriptExtraPaths": []
    },
    "Ruby": {
        "ruby": "/usr/bin/ruby",
        "rubyExtraPaths": []
    },
    "Python": {
        "python": '/usr/bin/python',
        "pythonExtraPaths": [
            "/usr/local/lib/python2.7/site-packages "
        ]
}}
```

Linting with SublimeLinter

Linting is a term for flagging suspicious and non-portable constructs, likely to be bugs in any written language. SublimeLinter is a plugin that supports linting and has the following linters built in:

- **C/C++**: This lints via `cppcheck`
- **CoffeeScript**: This lints `via coffee -s -l`
- **CSS**: This lints via built-in `csslint`
- **Haml**: This checks syntax via `haml -c`
- **HTML**: This lints via `tidy`
- **Java**: This lints via `javac -Xlint`
- **JavaScript**: This lints via built in `jshint`, `jslint`, or `gjslint` (if installed)
- **Lua**: This checks syntax via `luac`
- **Objective-J**: This lints via built in `capp_lint`
- **Perl**: This lints via `Perl::Critic` or syntax and deprecation check via `perl-c`
- **PHP**: This checks syntax via `php -l`
- **Puppet**: This checks syntax via `puppet parser validate`
- **Python**: This is a native, moderately-complete lint
- **Ruby**: This checks syntax via `ruby -wc`
- **XML**: This lints via `xmllint`

Installing SublimeLinter

We can install this plugin by using the Package Control that we installed earlier. Let's open it by pressing *Ctrl + Shift + P* in Windows or Linux and *command + Shift + P* in OS X; choose **Install Package** and install the **SublimeLinter** plugin.

Using SublimeLinter

SublimeLinter can run in four different modes; the current mode is set by the `sublimelinter` key in the user settings:

- **Background mode (default)**: When the `sublimelinter` key is set to `true`, linting is performed constantly in the background while we modify the file.
- **Load-save mode**: When the `sublimelinter` key is set to `load-save`, linting will be performed when a file is loaded and after the file is saved.

- **Save-only mode**: When the `sublimelinter` key is set to `save-only`, linting is performed only after a file is saved.
- **On demand Mode**: When the `sublimelinter` key is set to `false`, linting will only be initiated by us. We can initiate a lint by pressing *Ctrl + Alt + L* on Windows or Linux and *Control + command + L* on OS X.

We can also control all SublimeLinter settings and initiate an instant lint from the `command` **palette. Press** *Ctrl + Shift + P* **or** *command + Shift + P* **and type** `SublimeLinter:` **; you will see all the options for quick linting and quick mode changing.**

Configuring SublimeLinter

There are a number of customizations that SublimeLinter supports:

- Custom Linters
- Per project settings
- Customizing colors

We won't cover these customizations in this book, but we can always go to `https://github.com/SublimeLinter/SublimeLinter`, and learn more about them.

The must-know shortcuts map

The following is a must-know shortcuts map for Sublime Text:

General

General shortcuts for Sublime's basic features are as follows:

Command	Windows/Linux	OS X
Open the command palette	*Ctrl + Shift + P*	*command + Shift + P*
Toggle Side Bar	*Ctrl + KB*	*command + KB*
Show scope in status bar	*Ctrl + Shift + Alt + P*	*Control + Shift + P*
Python Console	*Ctrl + `*	*Control + `*
New Window	*Ctrl + Shift + N*	*command + Shift + N*

Tabs

Shortcuts to control tabbing in Sublime:

Command	Windows/Linux	OS X
New Tab	*Ctrl + N*	*command + N*
Close Tab	*Ctrl + W*	*command + W*
Open last closed Tab	*Ctrl + Shift + T*	*command + Shift + T*
Next Tab	*Ctrl + Tab*	*Control + Tab*
Previous Tab	*Ctrl + Shift+Tab*	*Control + Shift + Tab*

Bookmarks

Bookmarks are similar to the favorites option while surfing in the Web; we can toggle bookmarks on lines and then jump between them. Here are the shortcuts for using Bookmarks:

Command	Windows/Linux	OS X
Toggle Bookmark	*Ctrl + F2*	*command + F2*
Next Bookmark	*F2*	*F2*
Previous Bookmark	*Shift + F2*	*Shift + F2*
Clear Bookmarks	*Ctrl + Shift + F2*	*command + Shift + F2*

Editing

All Sublime shortcuts that are related to editing text/code:

Command	Windows/Linux	OS X
Delete line	*Ctrl + X*	*command + X*
Insert line after	*Ctrl + Enter*	*command + Enter*
Insert line before	*Ctrl + Shift + Enter*	*command + Shift + Enter*
Move line Up/Down	*Ctrl + Shift +* the up/down arrow key	*command + Control +* the up/down arrow key
Select line	*Ctrl + L*	*command + L*
Select word	*Ctrl + D*	*command + D*
Jump to matching bracket	*Ctrl + M*	*Control + M*
Delete from cursor to end of line	*Ctrl + KK*	*command + KK*

Command	Windows/Linux	OS X
Delete from cursor to start of line	*Ctrl + K + backspace*	*command + K + backsapce*
Indent current lines	*Ctrl +]*	*command +]*
Un-indent current lines	*Ctrl + [*	*command + [*
Duplicate lines	*Ctrl + Shift + D*	*command + Shift + D*
Join lines	*Ctrl + J*	*command + J*
Toggle comment for current line	*Ctrl + /*	*command + /*
Block comment selection	*Ctrl + Shift + /*	*command + Option + /*
Undo	*Ctrl + Z*	*command + Z*
Redo	*Ctrl + Y*	*command + Y*
Soft Undo	*Ctrl + U*	*Control + U*
Soft Redo	*Ctrl + Shift + U*	*command + Shift + U*
Next auto-complete suggestion	*Ctrl + Space*	*Control + Space*
Paste and indent correctly	*Ctrl + Shift + V*	*command + Shift + V*

Summary

By now we should have mastered code editing and keyboard shortcuts; we can now work on any project in any language with the help of Lint and Code Intelligence.

It is important to know that SublimeLinter and SublimeCodeIntel do not support all kinds of projects and languages. They are also not the right choice for you if you are developing in a specific language; there may be a plugin that fits your requirement better. In the next chapter we are going to learn what Snippets, Macros, and Key Bindings are, and even make our own snippet!

3
Snippets, Macros, and Key Bindings

This chapter will help you to master snippet and macro skills and guide you through customizing and managing your key bindings. In this chapter we will cover the following topics:

- Getting to know a snippet
- Understanding your first snippet
- Using Package Control snippets
- Recording, editing, and using macros
- New key bindings

Getting to know a snippet

As developers, we all get to write the same short code fragments over and over again on different files and projects. The best example of this is the following code:

```html
<!DOCTYPE html>
<html>
  <head>
    <title> My cool Website </title>
  </head>
  <body>
    <p> Hello World! </p>
  </body>
</html>
```

We all have written something similar so many times. That's why Sublime has the snippets feature. Snippets are smart templates that insert the right text when we need it, where we need it.

Let's see this example live by using **Lorem ipsum**. We have this empty HTML page that we wrote using our awesome, fast fingers. Now we want to enter some placeholder text inside the <p> tags, as shown in the following screenshot:

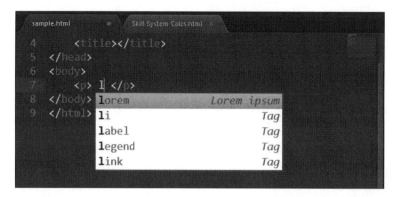

We just type the trigger letter for our snippet, in this case l, and we get all the options. Pressing *Tab* will insert the snippet as shown in the following screenshot:

```
sample.html        ●    Skill System Calcs.html  ×
4          <title></title>
5      </head>
6      <body>
7          <p> Lorem ipsum dolor sit amet, consectetur
           adipisicing elit, sed do eiusmod
8          tempor incididunt ut labore et dolore magna
           aliqua. Ut enim ad minim veniam,
9          quis nostrud exercitation ullamco laboris nisi
           ut aliquip ex ea commodo
10         consequat. Duis aute irure dolor in
           reprehenderit in voluptate velit esse
11         cillum dolore eu fugiat nulla pariatur.
           Excepteur sint occaecat cupidatat non
12         proident, sunt in culpa qui officia deserunt
           mollit anim id est laborum. </p>
13     </body>
14     </html>
```

Yes! We now have a **Lorem ipsum**. We could also achieve this by writing lore and pressing *Ctrl* + space on Windows, Linux, and OS X. Because we do not have other snippets starting with lore, Sublime will know exactly what we meant.

Understanding your first snippet

We learned that snippets can be very helpful, so how about creating our own? We'll make an awesome HTML snippet, better than the one in the preceding example. First, let's have a look at how snippets work in more detail.

How do snippets work?

Snippets can be saved under any package folder, but we'll start with saving our snippets under `Packages/User`. Snippets must live in a Sublime package.

File format and syntax

Snippets are simple XML-formatted files with the extension `sublime-snippet`. The root XML tag will always be `<snippet>` and will then contain the following:

- `Content`: This tag represents the actual snippet.
    - If we want to write $, we'll need to escape it with `\$`.
    - For indentation, use tabs only. If the `translate_tabs_to_spaces` option is set to `true`, tabs will be transformed to spaces automatically when the snippet is inserted.
    - The `Content` tag must contain the `<![CDATA[...]]>` section. Snippets won't work if we won't do it.
    - Also, the `Content` tag cannot contain `]]>` because these three characters will close the `<!CDATA[...]]>` section, and this will cause an XML error. A cool workaround for this is placing an undefined variable, for example, `]]$UNDEFINED_VAR>`. The XML parser will replace any undefined variables with empty strings.
- `tabTrigger`: This tag contains a sequence of characters that will trigger the snippet when written. After writing these characters, pressing *Tab* will insert the snippet immediately.
- `Scope`: This is the scope in which the snippet will be active.
    - To get our current scope, press *Ctrl* + *Shift* + *Alt* + *P* on Windows/ Linux and *Control* + *Shift* + *P* on OS X, and then check the status bar for the current scope.
    - All Sublime Text 3 scopes can be found at `http://gist.github. com/danpe/6993237`.
- `Description`: A short and intuitive description for the snippet, which will be shown when the snippet's menu is open.

`ScopeHunter` is a great plugin when working with scopes; we can install it from Package Control.

Knowing about snippets' features

Snippets have some extra features that can be really helpful such as inserting copyrights on code, inserting default file structures, or just helping us type functions faster. We will cover all that you need to know about snippets so that you can take full advantage of them.

Environment variables

We learned about Sublime's environment variables in a previous chapter. Snippets can also access these variables, which can be very convenient as shown in the following example:

```
$TM_FILENAME - Filename of current file
$TM_LINE_NUMBER - Current row
```

The full list of Sublime Text environment variables can be found at `http://gist.github.com/danpe/6996806`.

Field markers

Field Markers will let us cycle between our snippet's field markers by pressing *Tab*. We'll use fields for customizing a snippet after it's been inserted.

Mirrored field markers

Identical field markers mirror what we write on one of them. When we edit the first mirrored field marker, the rest will change in real time to the same values.

Placeholders

We can even put some default values, which are called placeholders. Let's see a full example of field markers' usage:

```
Hello ${1:$TM_FULLNAME}!
We are $2, The best Snippets Team!
$2 Helps making snippets since 1999.
```

As we can see in this example, the cursor will start on $1 with a default value of an environment variable. Cool! We can put any value though. Next, the cursor will jump to the $2 on the second line and will mirror the value we write to $2 in the third line.

Creating our first snippet

We are going to make a cool HTML5 structure snippet. Let's go to **Tools | New Snippet...** and Sublime will open a new snippet template for us, as shown in the following screenshot:

Move the cursor over the commented line and remove the comments easily by pressing *Ctrl + /* on Windows or Linux and *Command + /* on OS X. Let's have a look at the following code:

```
<snippet>
  <content><![CDATA[<!doctype html>
<html>
  <head>
    <meta charset="utf-8">
    <meta name="description" content="$1">
    <meta name="viewport" content="width=device-width, initial
scale=1">
    <title>${2:Untitled}</title>
  </head>
  <body>
    Hello ${3:$TM_FULLNAME}! Welcome to $2!
    $0
  </body>
</html>]]>
  </content>
  <tabTrigger>doctype</tabTrigger>
  <description>HTML5 Structure</description>
  <scope>text.html</scope>
</snippet>
```

The good thing about snippets is that they are self-explanatory, but we'll still go over this one.

Writing `doctype` in a `.html` file and pressing *Tab* will insert the snippet and the cursor will jump to fill in the description `meta` tag. Pressing *Tab* again will make the cursor jump to fill in the `title`, which is filled with a default value of `Untitled`. The value that we'll insert will be mirrored inside the body on variable `$2`. Pressing *Tab* again will take the cursor to fill variable `$3`, which has the default value of an environment variable. Pressing *Esc* at any time will take us to the snippet's exit point which is variable `$0`, or the end of the snippet, if not specified. We can also go backward while editing a field by pressing *Shift* + *Tab*. Let's save this file inside `Packages/User/doctype.sublime-snippet`.

We can now open any `.html` file and use our snippet, as shown in the following screenshot:

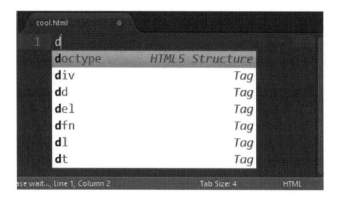

Pressing *Enter/Tab* will result in the following:

```
cool.html
1  <!doctype html>
2  <html>
3      <head>
4          <meta charset="utf-8">
5          <meta name="description" content="|">
6          <meta name="viewport" content="width=device-width, initial scale=1">
7          <title>Untitled</title>
8      </head>
9      <body>
10          Hello ! Welcome to Untitled!
11
12      </body>
13  </html>
```

Using Package Control snippets

We can spend all day long writing snippets, or we can find awesome snippets created by Sublime's awesome community.

Just like installing any other plugin, we can go to **Install Package** and look for snippets' packages. Here are some packages I recommend you use for web development:

Package name	Languages
EvercodeLab Sublime snippets	Ruby on Rails, ERB, Symfony 2
Additional PHP snippets	PHP
jQuery snippets pack	jQuery
Twitter Bootstrap snippets	Twitter Bootstrap
AngularJS	AngularJS
HTML snippets	HTML
JavaScript snippets	JavaScript

To find more awesome snippets go to `https://sublime.wbond.net/browse/labels/snippets`.

Recording, editing, and using macros

Macros can be very helpful; they are saved with the `.sublime-macro` extensions as a JSON-formatted file.

Before creating a new macro, we should understand what the use case is. If we find ourselves doing the same actions over and over again, we should use a macro for it. For example, when writing **C#** code, we always go to the end of the line to insert a semicolon and press *Enter*. How can we do this faster?

Recording a macro

To record a macro, simply press *Ctrl + Q* on Windows or Linux and *Control + Q* on OS X. We will notice that the status bar says **Starting to record macro...**, as shown in the following screenshot:

Line 1, Column 1; Starting to record macro...   Tab Size: 4   C#

Let's record the macro. Press *Ctrl* + right arrow + ; + *Enter* on Windows or Linux and *Command* + Right Arrow + ; + *Return* on OS X. Finally, press *Ctrl* + *Q* to stop recording.

```
Line 2, Column 1; Recorded macro with 3 commands                    Tab Size: 4                    C#
```

Playing a macro

To play the recorded macro, simply press *Ctrl* + *Shift* + *Q* on Windows or Linux and *Control* + *Shift* + *Q* on OS X. Sublime will always play the last recorded macro.

Saving and editing

We can also save the recorded macro and edit it manually. Let's go to **Tools | Save Macro...** and save it under `Packages/User/semicolon.sublime-macro`. When opened open it for editing, we should see the following:

```
[
    { "args": { "to": "eol" }, "command": "move_to" },
    { "args": { "characters": ";" }, "command": "insert" },
    { "args": { "characters": "\n" }, "command": "insert" }
]
```

We can edit the macro to insert) ; instead of ; just by changing the value of `"characters"` in the second row to `");"`.

For the full list of commands, visit `http://docs.sublimetext.info/en/sublime-text-3/reference/commands.html`.

Binding a saved macro

We recorded, saved, and edited our macro. Now, we want to make it accessible for later use, and one way of doing this is by binding the macro to a shortcut key. We will do this by defining a new key binding to our macro.

New key bindings

Let's open the user default key bindings by going to **Preferences | Key Bindings-User**. This will open a new file (should be an empty JSON array) named `Default (OS).sublime-keymap`, where OS is replaced with our operating system.

Let's add the following line to the array:

```
{ "keys": ["super+alt+;"], "command": "run_macro_file",
  "args": {"file": "Packages/User/semicolon.sublime-macro"} }
```

This line will run the macro that is located in `Packages/User` and is named `semicolon.sublime-macro` when pressing *Super + Alt + ;*, *Super* is **WinKey** in Windows or Linux and *Command* on OS X. Our file should look like the following screenshot:

```
Default (Windows).sublime-keymap

1   [
2        { "keys": ["super+alt+;"], "command": "run_macro_file",
3            "args": {"file": "Packages/User/semicolon.sublime-macro"} }
4   ]
5
```

Once you save this file, you can run the macro using the specified shortcut.

All commands used by shortcuts are the same commands that are used by the macros.

Summary

We are stocked with snippets, both our own and from the community. We have recorded a macro, saved it, and bound it to a shortcut key.

In the next chapter we are going to learn about overriding existing key bindings and how to avoid collisions. We will also learn how to customize Sublime's base settings, Colors, and Themes. We'll even create our own theme.

And for dessert, we will play with Splitting Windows in Sublime.

4

Customization and Theme Development

This chapter will give us the ability to fully customize our Sublime Text's look and feel. We will also customize our own color theme. And as a bonus, we will check out the Split Windows feature.

In this chapter we will cover the following topics:

- Overriding and maintaining key bindings
- Understanding Sublime's base settings
- Beautifying Sublime with colors and themes
- Mastering Split Windows

Overriding and maintaining key bindings

In the previous chapter, we bound as key combination to our macro. Sublime also gives us the option to bind keys to any command by adding custom key bindings; but what are key bindings exactly? In one sentence:

"Key bindings map key presses to commands."

All of Sublime's key bindings are configurable by JSON-formatted `.sublime-keymap` files.

Platform-specific key bindings

Key bindings can be different per platform; their filename has to be one of the following:

- `Default (Windows).sublime-keymap`

- `Default (OSX).sublime-keymap`

- `Default (Linux).sublime-keymap`

These file names are platform dependent; this means that the key bindings defined in the Windows `keymap` file will only work if we are on Windows or other OSes. It is important to know that user-specified key bindings need to be placed in `Packages/User/Default (<platform>).sublime-keymap`.

Key map file structure

A key map is an array of key bindings. Each key binding contains the following elements:

- `keys`: This contains an array of case-sensitive keys that needs to be pressed to trigger the key binding. We can make chords by using an array, for example, `["ctrl+k", "ctrl+b"]`.

- `command`: This contains the command to be executed.

- `args` (optional): This contains a dictionary of parameters to be passed to the `command` element.

- `context` (optional): This contains an array of contexts that will enable the key binding. All contexts must be `true` for the key binding to be enabled.

Here's an example from the Windows default key map:

```
[
    { "keys": ["ctrl+n"], "command": "new_file" },
    { "keys": ["ctrl+shift+n"], "command": "new_window" }
]
```

The first key binding will open a new tab when *Ctrl + N* is pressed, and the second key binding will open a new window when *Ctrl + Shift + N* is pressed.

 For a list of all available commands, visit either `http://gist.github.com/danpe/7189451` or `http://docs.sublimetext.info/en/sublime-text-3/reference/commands.html`.

Bindable keys

Sublime supports almost all keyboard keys as bindable keys. Here is the full list of all the keyboard keys that can be used with key bindings:

Up	down	right	left	insert	browser_back
home	end	pageup	pagedown	backspace	browser_forward
delete	tab	enter	pause	escape	browser_refresh
space	keypad0	keypad1	keypad2	keypad3	browser_search
keypad4	keypad5	keypad6	keypad7	keypad8	browser_stop
keypad9	clear	f1	f2	f3	browser_home
f4	f5	f6	f7	f8	browser_favorites
f9	f10	f11	f12	f13	keypad_period
f14	f15	f16	f17	f18	keypad_divide
f19	f20	sysreq	break	shift	keypad_multiply
ctrl	alt	super	context_menu	keypad_plus	keypad_minus

We have some restrictions though. On Windows, we should not use *Ctrl + Alt +* an alphanumeric key, while on OS X, we should not use *Option +* an alphanumeric key Number keys cannot be bound. For example, we cannot use *Ctrl+7*.

Advanced key bindings

Simple key bindings include only BoundKeys and a command. However, we can also make more advanced key bindings by passing arguments to the command using the args key; for example:

```
{ "keys": ["enter"], "command": "insert", "args": {"characters": "\n"}
}
```

In this key binding, we pass \n to the insert command when we press *Enter*. More advanced key bindings can be achieved using contexts. A context determines if the command will be executed based on the caret's position or some other state. For example:

```
{ "keys": ["escape"], "command": "hide_auto_complete", "context":
    [
        { "key": "auto_complete_visible", "operator": "equal",
```

```
    "operand": true }
      ]
}
```

This key binding will hide autocomplete when *Esc* is pressed, but only if autocomplete is visible; if not, this command won't get triggered.

 For a list of all available contexts, visit either `http://gist.github.com/danpe/7189722` or `http://docs.sublimetext.info/en/sublime-text-3/reference/key_bindings.html`.

Keeping our key bindings organized

A big problem is that Sublime keeps track of all the key bindings we have. So first, let's understand how Sublime knows when a key binding needs to override another key binding.

Sublime will start loading all the key bindings located in `Packages/Default`; then, it will sort all the installed packages in an alphabetic order and load them one after another. The last one to be loaded will always be `Packages/User`. Each `keymap` file that is being loaded will override any other key bindings that have been loaded before it in case of a key conflict. This means that `Packages/User` will override all the key bindings because it is being loaded last.

 Don't be afraid to read the preceding information twice. It's important to know how Sublime handles key bindings.

Lucky for us, we have an awesome plugin that can help us manage our key bindings and detect collisions and conflict. It is called **BoundKey**, and can be installed using our favorite Package Control! Let's open up the command palette by pressing *Ctrl + Shift + P* in Windows or Linux and *Command + Shift + P* in OS X. Then, we'll choose **Install Package** and install the BoundKeys plugin.

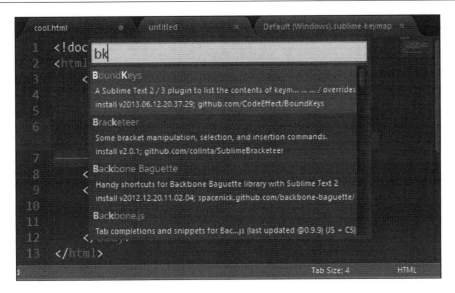

After installing it, we simply need to press *Shift + F10* to get a full, detailed list of all the BoundKeys and conflicts, if any.

 The FindKeyConflicts plugin is also recommended, and can be found at `https://github.com/skuroda/FindKeyConflicts`.

Understanding Sublime's base settings

As we saw, Sublime Text can be fully customized to fit our needs. It stores its settings in JSON-formatted `.sublims-settings` files. Sublime will load these settings files in the same order that it loads the `keymap` files. This means that our settings that are stored in `Packages/User` will always override all other settings except those that have been changed in the current buffer.

The types of settings' files

Each settings file has a prefix that defines its purpose. These prefixes are names that can be descriptive, such as `Preferences (Windows).sublime-settings`. This means that the file applies only to Windows. We can also specify the file type in the descriptive name, for example, `Ruby.sublime-settings`. This means that the file applies only when editing Ruby code files.

Customization walkthrough

In this section, we are going to customize Sublime to fit our coding style. Feel free to change the settings with whatever fits your style.

Adding packages

Let's start with adding some basic packages; download and install the following:

- `SideBarEnhancements`: This package adds useful file operations to the sidebar, such as a new file or new folder.

- `TrailingSpaces`: We all hate trailing whitespaces in our code! This package strips trailing whitespaces from our files.

We can install these packages using Package Control.

Tabs and spaces

Now, let's open Sublime's settings. We can choose which file we want to edit. If we want to edit Sublime's global settings, we will open it by navigating to **Preferences | Settings | Default**, and if we want to edit specific user settings, we will open it by navigating to **Preferences | Settings-User**. Add/change the following code:

```
{
    "tab_size": 2,
    "translate_tab_to_spaces": true
}
```

If you installed the `TrailingSpaces` package, it is recommended that you add the following code to the global settings:

```
"trim_trailing_white_space_on_save": true
```

Now every time we save a file, `TrailingSpaces` will remove all the trailing whitespaces from our file.

> For a full list of the settings, visit `http://docs.sublimetext.info/en/sublime-text-3/reference/settings.html`.

Beautifying Sublime with colors and themes

Sublime Text can be a beauty! We can change Sublime's visual experience by changing its base settings, color schemes, and themes.

Visual settings

Let's start by tweaking Sublime's settings to change visual elements; for example, we can highlight the current line, change the caret style, show fold buttons, boldface folder names, and highlight modified tabs. We are going to do this by opening our user preferences and adding some visual settings to it. The following numbered bullets refer to the labels on the next screenshot:

1. **"highlight_line": true, "caret_style": "phase"**
2. **"fade_fold_buttons": false**
3. **"bold_folder_labels": true**
4. **"highlight_modified_tabs": true**

The following screenshot shows the output of the visual settings:

This is cool but not enough for us; we want Sublime to be more awesome!

Sublime themes

Themes are JSON-formatted files with a `.sublime-theme` extension. Sublime themes modify Sublime's look and feel by changing icons and IDE colors.

Let's try downloading and installing the most popular theme, the soda theme, online. It's easy to install using Package Control. Open the command palette by pressing *Ctrl + Shift + P* in Windows or Linux and *Command + Shift + P* in OS X. Choose **Install Package** and install the **Theme - Soda** package. After installing the theme, we need to activate it. Let's open the user settings again by navigating to **Preferences | Settings | User** and add either `"theme": "Soda Light 3.sublime-theme"` for the light theme or `"theme": "Soda Dark 3.sublime-theme"` for the dark one. Also, we'll add `"soda_folder_icons": true` for the custom folder icons.

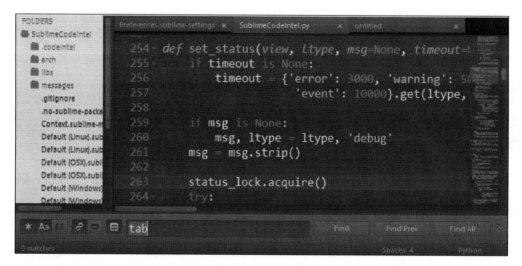

Wow! The folder icons, tabs styles, and search icons have been changed! Everything looks sleek. But now, we wish to change the colors.

Color schemes

Color schemes are XML-formatted files with a `.tmTheme` extension; they are located at `Packages/Color Scheme - Default` and can be changed at any time from the Sublime menu in **Preferences | Color Scheme | Theme**. Color schemes are an awesome way to fully customize Sublime's colors, while themes alter the UI Elements only. Let's try changing our color scheme to **Sunburst** by going to **Preferences | Color Scheme | Sunburst**.

We can also download custom color themes from the Web and install them by placing the `.tmTheme` files inside `Packages/User`. They will show up in Sublime's menu automatically.

The best way to create our custom color scheme is using this great online tool available at `http://tmtheme-editor.herokuapp.com`.

A recommended color scheme is the neon color scheme that aims to make as many languages as possible look as good a possible with bright colors on black colors. It can be installed through Package Control or can be found at `https://github.com/MattDMo/Neon-color-scheme`.

Mastering Split Windows

Sublime Text includes one of the most useful productivity features that is out there—Split Windows! We all know this from vi and Visual Studio, but how can we split our Sublime? We simply need to memorize some shortcut keys.

Let's split our window into two columns using *Alt + Shift + 2* on Windows or Linux and *Option + Command + 2* on OS X as shown in the following screenshot:

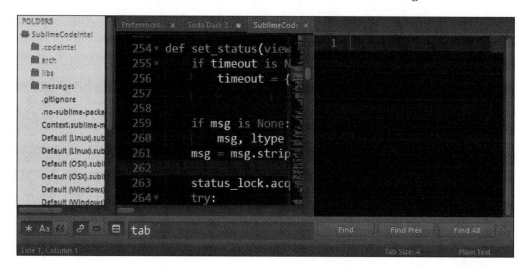

We got a new empty column. Now, we need to move a file there. We'll do it by pressing *Ctrl + Shift + 2* on Windows or Linux and *Control + Shift + 2* on OS X as shown in the following screenshot:

This feature is very useful when working with source and header files, or even when comparing two files. We can also open up a grid by pressing *Alt + Shift + 5* on Windows or Linux and *Option + Command + 5* on OS X as shown in the following screenshot:

To master this skill, we'll need to memorize the following shortcuts:

Split Windows shortcuts	Windows/Linux	OS X
Single window	*Alt + Shift + 1*	*Option + Command + 1*
Two to four columns	*Alt + Shift + [2/3/4]*	*Command + Option + [2/3/4]*
Two rows	*Alt + Shift + 8*	*Command + Option + 8*
Three rows	*Alt + Shift + 9*	*Command + Option + 9*
Grid, Two columns, Two rows	*Alt + Shift + 5*	*Command + Option + 5*
Move current file to group #	*Ctrl + Shift + [1/3/4]*	*Control + Shift + [1/3/4]*
Focus group #	*Ctrl + [1/2/3/4]*	*Control + [1/3/4]*

Summary

By the end of this chapter, we have a beautiful, customized Sublime Text application! We have learned how to bind keys to custom actions and how to split Sublime into rows and columns.

The next chapter is for the vi fans among us; we will introduce Sublime's Vintage feature and learn how we can make Sublime more like vi.

5
Unravelling Vintage Mode

This chapter is for the vi fans among us. In this chapter, we will cover the following topics:

- Understanding Vintage Mode
- Setting up Vintage Mode
- Experiencing Vintage Mode
- Knowing about Vintageous

Understanding Vintage Mode

Vintage Mode is a package that gives Sublime the editing features of vi. It allows us to use vi's commands while also having the advantage of Sublime's features, such as multiple selections that we learned before. Vintage Mode is an open source project and can be found at `http://github.com/sublimehq/Vintage`.

Discovering vi

vi is a an old but still very popular text editor. vi was originally created for Unix operating systems. The original vi was written in 1976 as an open source project. Surprisingly, it's still being used today because of its speed, small size, and portability. It is a popular command line editor (for example, in server environments) because it does not require a mouse.

Many different vi ports have been developed since its original release. One of the most popular of them is **vim** (**vi improved**), which supports customization like Sublime does, with macros, plugins, and key mappings.

The following is a screenshot of a spilt-windowed vi screen, which is not as great as our customized Sublime:

Setting up Vintage Mode

Vintage Mode is installed by default but is also disabled by default via the `ignored_packages` settings that is set in **User Preferences**. To enable the Vintage Mode, we'll need to remove it from the ignore packages list. To do this, let's open the user settings by going to **Preferences | Settings–User**. The following code is present in the user settings:

```
"ignored_packages":
[
"Vintage"
]
```

We will change the preceding code to the following one:

```
"ignored_packages": []
```

We have just enabled Vintage Mode! We should see **INSERT MODE** at the status bar. Insert Mode is the mode where we can type freely.

Experiencing Vintage Mode features

In this section, we are going to cover some vi commands, basic interactions, and usage of the Vintage Mode. If you have used vi before, you can skip this section.

Vintage Mode will start in **INSERT MODE** by default instead of **COMMAND MODE**; to change this behavior, we'll need to open up user settings again by going to **Preferences | Settings–User** and then adding the following code:

```
"vintage_start_in_command_mode": true
```

Don't worry if you are still confused about Insert Mode and Command Mode by the end of this chapter, you will understand it all.

Vintage editing modes

Vintage has four supported modes that can be switched between:

Mode	Description	Key
Command Mode	Waits for the user to enter a command	*Esc*
Insert Mode	Text can be inserted in different positions	*i/I/a/A*
Visual Mode	Select/highlight the text using the Movement Commands	*V*
Visual Line Mode	Select/highlight lines of text using the arrow keys	*Shift + V*

Vintage Mode commands

Vintage Mode includes most vi commands, though Ex commands are not implemented. The only exceptions are :w and :e, which work from the command palette.

For example, if we wish to copy three lines, we will use the Yank command which is bound to the *y* key and press 3 for repeating the Yank command three times. This will copy 3 lines forward from the current cursor position. The status bar will show **COMMAND MODE - Yank * 3**.

COMMAND MODE - Yank * 3, Line 5, Column 2   Tab Size: 4   JSON

To paste what we just copied, we'll press the *p* key. Mastering Vintage takes time and effort, but it's worth it!

Here are the vi commands that are supported by Vintage Mode.

Commands for changing modes

The following list contains all the shortcuts that enable us to switch between different modes:

Command description	Screen name	Bound key
Go back to Command Mode	**COMMAND MODE**	*Esc*
Insert at the current cursor position	**INSERT MODE**	*i*
Insert after the current cursor position	**INSERT MODE**	*a*
Insert at the beginning of the current line	**INSERT MODE**	*I*
Insert at the end of the current line	**INSERT MODE**	*A*
Change to Visual Mode	**VISUAL MODE**	*v*
Change to Visual Line Mode	**VISUAL LINE MODE**	*V*

Movement commands

The following list contains all the movement commands that help us navigate in Sublime while using Vintage Mode. These commands are the most important commands to remember, and they will boost our productivity while using Vintage Mode. These commands will not work in Insert Mode.

Command description	Bound key
Move left	*h*
Move down	*j*
Move up	*k*
Move right	*l*
Move to the end of the file	*G*
Move to the beginning of the file	*gg*
Move forward a paragraph.	*}*
Move backward a paragraph	*{*
Move to the next word	*w*
Move to the previous word	*b*
Move to the end of the line	*$*
Move to the beginning of the line	*^*
Move to the matching bracket	*%*
Move to the next occurrence of the current word	***

For better practice with the movement commands, it is recommended to install **VintageLines** using Package Control.

Editing commands

We can append most of the editing commands with a movement command, just like we appended Yank with 3, where 3 means three lines; we could also appended it with *G* for end of file.

Command description	Screen name	Bound key
Delete	**Delete**	d
Delete the whole current line	**Delete**	dd
Delete the character on the current position		x
Copy	**Yank**	y
Copy the whole current line	**Yank**	yy
Paste the current Yank		p
Lowercase	**Lower Case**	gu
Uppercase	**Upper Case**	$
Swap case	**Swap Case**	^
Indent	**Indent**	>
Unindent	**Unindent**	<
Open search box for searching forward		/
Open search box for searching backwards		?

In the preceding table, Delete, Copy, Lowercase, Uppercase, Swap case, Indent, Unindent commands can be appended with a Movement command.

Knowing about Vintageous

Sublime's default Vintage Mode is a little outdated as well as VintageEx Mode, which is only supported by Sublime Text 2, not 3. That's why Guillermo (@guillermooo) created its own Vintage package for Sublime Text 3, which emulates vi/vim more closely than the normal Vintage Mode.

Vintageous can be downloaded using Package Control, but we must first disable the default Sublime's Vintage Mode so Vintageous can take over.

We do this by adding back `"Vintage"` to `"ignored_packages"`; don't worry, all we learned about Vintage Mode still applies for Vintageous.

> For full information, visit the following link:
>
> `https://github.com/guillermooo/Vintageous`

Summary

In this chapter, we have discovered what vi/vim is and the fact that we can use it freely with all the shortcuts we mastered. It is important to know that vi functionality is huge and never-ending; hence, it can't be covered in one chapter and needs a whole book for it. We covered the basics.

I recommend having the vi graphical cheat sheet that can be found at `http://www.viemu.com/a_vi_vim_graphical_cheat_sheet_tutorial.html`. Keeping a copy under your keyboard can be really helpful.

The next chapter will guide us on how to use Sublime for testing with several languages such as PHP and Ruby.

6
Testing Using Sublime

This chapter will teach us how to use Sublime Text for testing our code in different languages.

The following topics will be covered in this chapter:

- Introduction to testing in Sublime Text
- Testing in PHP development
- Testing in Python development
- Testing in Ruby development

Introduction to testing in Sublime Text

Every programmer makes mistakes; the difference between a good programmer and a bad programmer is that a good programmer tests their code before releasing it. This makes the programmer detect issues and bugs as soon as possible and fix them before something goes wrong. Also, the sooner we fix a bug the less time and cost it takes from us.

Sublime Text doesn't have any built-in features to help us test our code while developing in different languages, but the community has made plugins that work with standard testing packages for the most commonly used languages. We can use those plugins to ease our code-testing. We will cover the following plugins: **PHPUnit** for PHP, **Unittest** for Python, and **RubyTest** for Ruby.

Testing in PHP development

For the PHP developers among us who test their code using PHPUnit, Sublime has an awesome plugin to support PHPUnit known as **sublime-phpunit,** written by *Stuart Herbert* and located at `http://github.com/stuartherbert/sublime-phpunit`.

Knowing about PHPUnit

If you are a PHP developer and do not know what PHPUnit is, you should learn that PHPUnit is "the standard" for unit testing in PHP projects. It combines a framework that lets us easily write and run tests with the facility to analyze the results.

We can learn more about PHPUnit at `https://github.com/sebastianbergmann/phpunit/` or check the full manual at `http://phpunit.de/manual/current/en/index.html`.

Using PHPUnit plugin for Sublime

Before using this plugin, we must have PHPUnit installed and functional in our project and know how to use it, a topic which is not covered here. We'll then need to download and install the PHPUnit plugin using Package Control. Let's open up the command palette by pressing *Ctrl + Shift + P* in Windows or Linux and *Command + Shift + P* in OS X. Then choose **Install Package** and install **PHPUnit** package. After installing it, we can right-click on our code to see the new the **PHPUnit** option that has been added to our context menu, as shown in the following screenshot:

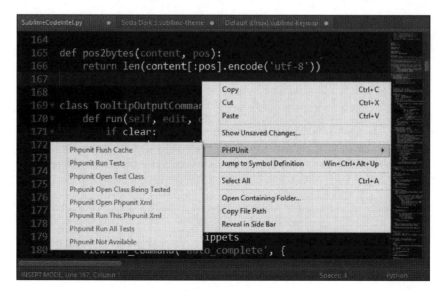

The options in **PHPUnit** are disabled because we are not currently inside a PHP project. To use the PHPUnit plugin in our project, we'll need a `phpunit.xml` or `phpunit.xml.dist` file. These files contain all the PHPUnit configuration options. PHPUnit will always favor `phpunit.xml` over `phpunit.xml.dist` if both exist. After your project is properly configured, right-clicking inside a source file should show the following:

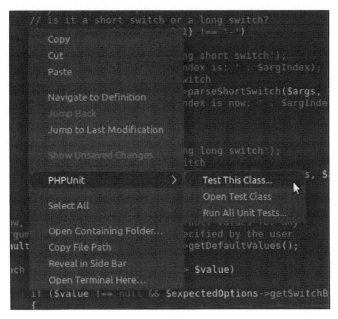

Stuart Herbert ©

As we can see in the preceding screenshot, we have three available options in the **PHPUnit** menu:

- **Test This Class…**: This option will run the unit tests just for this class.

- **Open Test Class**: This option opens our tests in Sublime Text; if tests are already open in Sublime this will switch between test's tabs.

- **Run All Unit Tests…**: This option runs all the unit tests for our code. This option just points to our `phpunit.xml` file.

> Test file names must match the original file names; for example, if our class is called `OurNamespace\OurClass.php`, the plugin expects to find our tests in a file called `OurNamespace\OurClassTest.php` somewhere inside our project.

We can also find all the available PHPUnit commands inside the command palette by pressing *Ctrl + Shift + P* on Windows or Linux and *Command + Shift + P* on OS X, and type phpunit, as shown in the following screenshot:

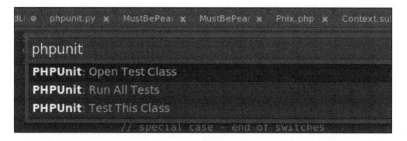

In the preceding screenshot, we can see all available commands that the PHPUnit plugin has to offer.

Helpful PHPUnit snippets

The PHPUnit plugin also includes some very helpful snippets to use while writing our unit tests:

- **phpunit-testcase**: This will create a new test class for us to fill out
- **phpunit-test**: This will create a new test method for us to fill out

These snippets can be used like any regular snippet, by typing their names and pressing the *Tab* key.

Testing in Python development

Python offers us **unittest**, an official unit testing framework for Python, sometimes referred as **PyUnit**. It's like a Python version of **JUnit** for Java and written by *Kent Beck* and *Erich Gamma*.

> For more information on how to use **unittest**, visit: http://docs.
> python.org/2/library/unittest.html

Currently the best package that helps us write Python unit tests is called **sublime-unittest** written by *Samuel Martin*, which can be found at https://github.com/martinsam/sublime-unittest.

Using unittest for Sublime

Python's unittest for Sublime is a package that contains a number of useful snippets to ease our unittest writing. To install the package, we'll use Package Control. Let's open the command palette by pressing *Ctrl + Shift + P* in Windows or Linux and *Command + Shift + P* in OS X. Then choose **Install Package** and install the **Unittest (python)** package.

The installed package has two main snippets:

- **testclass**: This will create a new test class for us to fill out

  ```
  class [Foo]TestCase(unittest.TestCase):
      ...
  ```

- **testfunc**: This will create a new test function for us to fill out

  ```
  def test_[foo](self):
      ...
  ```

After creating a test function, we'll need to use some assertions, which the package includes and also the following assertions snippets:

Snippet	Function	Checks that
asse	`assetEqual(first, second, msg=None)`	`first` = `second`
assne	`assertNotEqual(first, second, msg=None)`	`first` != `second`
asst	`assertTrue(expr, msg=None)`	`bool(expr)` is True
assf	`assertFalse(expr, msg=None)`	`bool(expr)` is False
assis	`assertIs(first, second, msg=None)`	`first` is `second`
assisnt	`assertIsNot(first, second, msg=None)`	`first` is not `second`
assisne	`assertIsNone(expr, msg=None)`	`expr` is None
assisntne	`assertIsNotNone(expr, msg=None)`	`expr` is not None
assin	`assertIn(first, second, msg=None)`	`first` in `second`
assnin	`assertNotIn(first, second, msg=None)`	`first` not in `second`
assisins	`assertIsInstance(obj, cls, msg=None)`	`isinstance(obj, cls)`
assnisins	`assertNotIsInstance(obj, cls, msg=None)`	`not isinstance(obj, cls)`

Let's try creating a new Test class using our snippets, starting with writing testclass and pressing *Tab* to insert the snippet. We'll call our TestSequenceFunctions class. We'll also create a test function called test_shuffle using the testfunc snippet, as shown in the following screenshot:

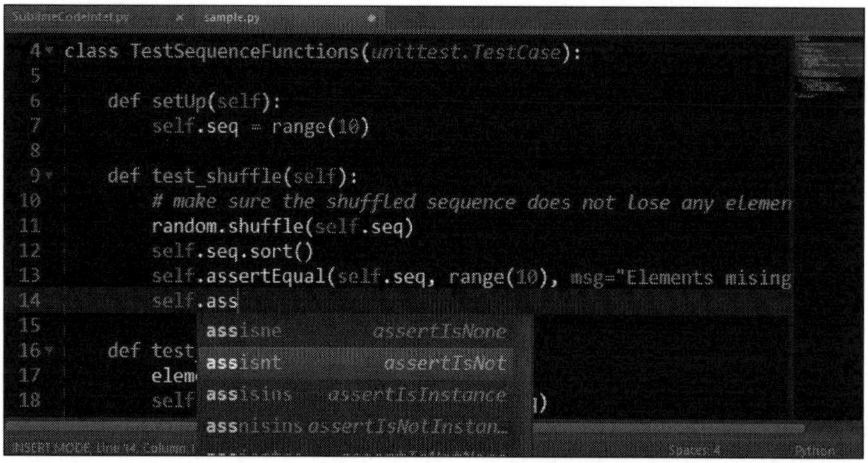

When inserting a snippet, we will get the preceding autocomplete window. Pressing *Tab* will insert the snippet.

```python
import random
import unittest

class TestSequenceFunctions(unittest.TestCase):

    def setUp(self):
        self.sequence = range(30)

    def test_shuffle(self):
        # checks that the shuffled sequence doesn't lose any elements
        # while shuffling and sorting
        random.shuffle(self.sequence)
        self.sequence.sort()
        self.assertEqual(self.sequence, range(30), msg="Elements missing")

if __name__ == '__main__':
    unittest.main()
```

When this code is executed, the `setUp` function is the first to be called and will initialize our `sequence`. After that, it will start to run all the test functions and assert if something goes wrong. The test functions `test_shuffle` or `random.shuffle(self.sequence)` will shuffle our sequence randomly, and then `self.sequence.sort()` will sort it back. Afterwards, we check if our sorted sequence is equal to `range(30)`, which returns a sorted sequence from `0` to `30`. If something went wrong and the sequence doesn't equal the range of `0` to `30`, then this test will fail with a message of **Elements missing**.

We can run this code as we run every Python code:

```
C:\Users\Danpe\Desktop>python sample.py
.
----------------------------------------------------------------
Ran 1 test in 0.000s

OK
```

The preceding is the result of a successful run of our test.

Testing in Ruby development

Ruby also has its built-in unit testing library called **Test::Unit**, but most people like using **Behavior-Driven Development (BDD)** when using Ruby, and Rails especially. There are two popular BBD frameworks: RSpec and Cucumber.

Quote from the `RSpec.info` website:

> *"RSpec is a testing tool for the Ruby programming language. Born under the banner of Behavior-Driven Development, it is designed to make Test-Driven Development a productive and enjoyable experience."*

Quote from the Cucumber repository:

> *"Cucumber is a tool that executes plain-text functional descriptions as automated tests."*

We are lucky that there is a single package for Sublime that supports the three testing frameworks: Test::Unit, RSpec, and Cucumber. It's called **RubyTest** and can be found on `https://github.com/maltize/sublime-text-2-ruby-tests`.

The package is called **sublime-text-2-ruby-tests** but it supports both Sublime Text 2 and 3.

Using RubyTest for Sublime

To install the **RubyTest** package, we'll use Package Control. Let's open the command palette by pressing *Ctrl + Shift + P* in Windows or Linux and *Command + Shift + P* in OS X. Choose **Install Package** and then install the **RubyTest** package. The **RubyTest** package doesn't include any snippets but has some useful commands instead. Here is a list of all the commands and their shortcuts:

RubyTest command	Windows/Linux	OS X
Run single test	*Ctrl + Shift + R*	*Command + Shift + R*
Run all tests from current file	*Ctrl + Shift + T*	*Command + Shift + T*
Run last test(s)	*Ctrl + Shift + E*	*Command + Shift + E*
Show test panel	*Ctrl + Shift + X*	*Command + Shift + X*
Check RB, ERB Syntax	*Alt + Shift + V*	*Option + Shift + V*

Here is how a testing result should look after being run using RubyTest:

![Screenshot of a Sublime Text window showing a Ruby test file and test results panel]

We can see that we received **2 assertions**, **1 failure**, and **0 errors**.

Supporting bundler

RubyTest also has a bundler autodetect feature that is based on the presence of a `Gemfile` in the `project root` directory. If this feature is enabled, RubyTest will automatically scan for the `Gemfile` and will add a prefix of `bundle exec` to any command it runs.

To enable this feature, we'll need to add a line to the RubyTest settings. We'll do it by going to **Preferences | Package Settings | RubyTest | Settings – User** and adding the following code:

```
{
    "check_for_bundler": true
}
```

After saving, the bundler autodetect feature is enabled.

Summary

In this chapter, we learned how to test our PHP, Python, and Ruby code using the best Sublime plugins.

In the next chapter, we will learn how to debug our PHP, JavaScript, and C/C++ code using the best plugins, all without leaving the Sublime environment!

7
Debugging Using Sublime

This chapter will teach us how to use Sublime Text for debugging our code in different languages. The following topics will be covered in this chapter:

- Introduction to debugging in Sublime Text
- Debugging PHP with Xdebug
- Debugging JavaScript with Web Inspector
- Debugging C/C++ with GDB

Introduction to debugging in Sublime Text

We'll start with a famous quote by *Steve McConnell*:

> *"It's hard enough to find an error in your code when you're looking for it; it's even harder when you've assumed your code is error-free."*

That is why we use debuggers to help us debug our code, find errors, and fix them. Sublime has some plugins that integrate some debugging features in them. We will cover debugging PHP using **SublimeTextXdebug**, debugging JavaScript using **SublimeWebInspector**, and debugging C/C++ using **SublimeGDB**.

> *"If debugging is the process of removing bugs, then programming must be the process of putting them in."*

> – *Edsger W. Dijkstra*

Debugging PHP with Xdebug

Xdebug is a PHP extension that provides us with debugging and profiling capabilities. It includes stack traces, real-time parameters' display, filenames, and line indicators. Sublime has a great plugin to help us debug our PHP code while using Xdebug. Having Xdebug installed is mandatory for this section; for more information, please visit: http://xdebug.org/docs/install.

Using Xdebug for Sublime

There are two Xdebug plugins for Sublime. We will install the Xdebug Client. To install the SublimeTextXdebug package, we'll use Package Control. Open the command palette by pressing *Ctrl + Shift + P* in Windows or Linux, and *Command + Shift + P* in OS X. Then choose **Install Package** and install the **Xdebug Client** package.

After installing, we'll need to change the xdebug.ini configuration file:

```
[xdebug]
zend_extension = "/absolute/path/to/our/xdebug-extension.so"
;zend_extension = "C:\Program Files (x86)\PHP\ext\php_xdebug.dll"
Xdebug.remote_enable = 1
Xdebug.remote_host = "127.0.0.1"
Xdebug.remote_port = 9000
Xdebug.remote_handler = "dbgp"
Xdebug.remote_mode = req
Xdebug.remote_connect_back = 1
```

If we are using a Linux/OS X platform, we should keep the Windows path commented and give an absolute path to our xdebug-extension.so file. If we are using Windows, we should comment the first line by adding a semicolon, uncomment the second one by removing the semicolon, and change the path to where our php_xdebug.dll file is located. We should restart the server after this.

The following screenshot is that of a debugging session:

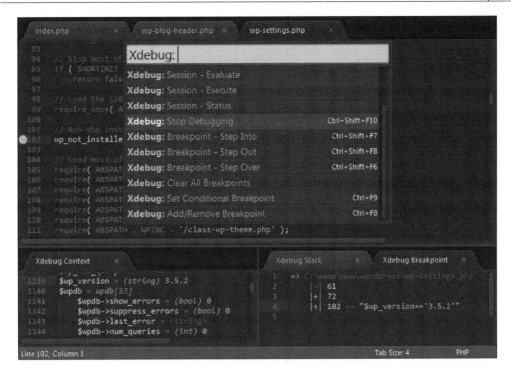

As we can see in the preceding screenshot, all available **Xdebug** commands are being shown on the command palette, and we have three new windows at the bottom:

- **Xdebug Context**: This window shows all variables in the current context
- **Xdebug Stack**: This window shows the current call stack
- **Xdebug Breakpoint**: This window shows all breakpoints that have been set

The following are all the commands that we will need to have for a good debugging session:

SublimeXdebug command	Windows/Linux	OS X
Start debugging	*Ctrl + Shift + F9*	*Command + Shift + F9*
Stop debugging	*Ctrl + Shift + F10*	*Command + Shift + F10*
Add/remove breakpoint	*Ctrl + F8*	*Command + F8*
Set conditional breakpoint	*Shift + F8*	*Shift + F8*
Run	*Ctrl + Shift + F5*	*Command + Shift + F5*
Step over	*Ctrl + Shift + F6*	*Command + Shift + F6*
Step into	*Ctrl + Shift + F7*	*Command + Shift + F7*
Step out	*Ctrl + Shift + F8*	*Command + Shift + F8*

All commands can also be found in the command palette by pressing *Ctrl + Shift + P* in Windows or Linux, and *Command + Shift + P* in OS X, or typing Xdebug: in the Sublime Text menu under **Tools | Xdebug**.

 If you are facing any trouble, try visiting the Troubleshoot page at: https://github.com/martomo/ SublimeTextXdebug#troubleshoot.

Debugging JavaScript with Web Inspector

There are tons of web developers among us, and we all find our own ways of debugging our JavaScript code. Sublime has a wonderful plugin to make it easy for us. It is called **Sublime Web Inspector (SWI)**. It lets us set breakpoints, examine the console, evaluate selections, debug step-by-step, and more! This plugin requires Google Chrome to be installed.

Installing Sublime Web Inspector

At the time this was written, the Package Control didn't include a Sublime Text 3 version of **SWI**. So, we'll need to install it manually by cloning the **ST3** branch on the **SWI** repository on GitHub. Let's start by opening our packages directory from the Sublime Text menu by navigating to **Preferences | Browse Packages...**. This will open up the packages directory. We'll need to navigate to this directory from the console; in Windows, we can do it simply by *Shift* + right-click | **Open command window here**, while on Linux and OS X, we'll need to use cd to navigate manually from the terminal. After we are in the packages directory, we need to clone the right branch by executing the following:

```
git clone -b ST3 "git://github.com/sokolovstas/SublimeWebInspector.git"
```

To test out the installation, we'll open the command palette and go to **Web Inspector | Start Google Chrome with remote debug port 9222**; this should open up Chrome. If we get an error message saying **The system cannot find the file specified**, we'll need to change the path for our chrome installation. We'll do it by going to the cloned directory and edit swi.sublime-settings to fit our needs:

```
// Path to google chrome
    "chrome_path": {
        "osx": "/Applications/Google Chrome.app/Contents/MacOS/Google
Chrome",
        "windows": "C:\\Users\\Danpe\\AppData\\Local\\Google\\Chrome\\
Application\\chrome.exe",
        "windows_x64": "C:\\Users\\Danpe\\AppData\\Local\\Google\\
Chrome\\Application\\chrome.exe",
        "linux": "/usr/bin/google-chrome"
    },
```

Make sure that all Chrome windows are closed before opening with the debug port and the path settings are correct. Chrome won't open in the debug mode if another Chrome window is already open.

Using Sublime Web Inspector (SWI)

After opening Chrome in the debug mode, we will call the Web Inspector again by pressing *Ctrl + Shift + R* on Windows or Linux, and *Command + Shift + R* on OS X. We should see the **Start debugging** and **Add/Remove Breakpoint** commands, as shown in the following screenshot:

Clicking on **Start debugging** will give us a list of all currently open tabs in Chrome. We'll choose the one that we wish to debug. We will see a screen similar to the following screenshot:

We can see all our debug prints as well as warnings and errors inside the console. While making a change and saving, the page will get auto refreshed. Let's try it by changing a to b where b isn't a real variable, and see what happens:

Oops! We got an error. We can see where the breakpoint stopped (**Resume, Step Over, Step Into,** and **Step Out**). We can also add our own breakpoint by calling the Web Inspector and clicking on **Add/Remove Breakpoint**. SWI exposes its commands so we can bind any keys to those commands. The following is a list of all the exposed commands:

Description	Command
Start debugger	`swi_debug_start`
Stop debugger	`swi_debug_stop`
Start Google Chrome	`swi_debug_start_chrome`
Show mapping of a local file to a URL	`swi_show_file_mapping`
Add/remove breakpoints	`swi_debug_breakpoint`
Resume from pause	`swi_debug_resume`
Step Into debugger	`swi_debugger_step_into`
Step Out debugger	`swi_debugger_step_out`
Step Over debugger	`swi_debug_step_over`
Evaluate selection	`swi_debug_evaluate`
Reload debugged page	`swi_debug_reload`

Debugging C/C++ with GDB

The **GNU Project Debugger** (**GDB**) is a debugger built by the open source GNU Project, and it lets us debug the following languages:

- Ada
- C
- C++
- D
- Fortran
- Go
- Modula-2
- Objective-C
- OpenCL C
- Pascal

GDB comes with most of the Unix distributions that include Linux and OS X. In the latest OS X named Maverick, GDB isn't installed by default and can be installed using **brew**. For Windows, we will have to download and install **Minimalist GNU for Windows** (**MinGW**) from `http://sourceforge.net/projects/mingw/files/`. This will let us compile C code and use GDB to debug it. Sublime has an awesome plugin called SublimeGDB, which is used for debugging with GDB, and is written by *Fredrik Ehnbom* (`@quarnster`).

Using SublimeGDB

We'll start by installing Sublime GDB using the Package Control. Let's open the command palette by pressing *Ctrl + Shift + P* in Windows or Linux, and *Command + Shift + P* in OS X. Then choose **Install Package** and install the **SublimeGDB** package. After installing, we'll need to configure SublimeGDB to make it work. Let's create a new Hello World C file, `hello.c`:

```c
#include <stdio.h>

int main(void)
{
    printf("Hello World!\n");
    return 0;
}
```

Make sure this is the only file in our current project, and save the project by going to **Project | Save Project As...** in the Sublime menu. After the project has been saved, let's edit it by going to **Project | Edit Project**. A new empty JSON project file will be opened. We'll need to add the following to make SublimeGDB work:

```json
{
    "folders":
    [
        {
            "path": "C:\\Users\\Danpe\\Desktop\\src",
        },
    ],
    "settings":
    {
        "sublimegdb_workingdir": "${folder:${project_path:hello.
exe}}",
        // NOTE: You MUST provide --interpreter=mi for the plugin to
work
        "sublimegdb_commandline": "gdb --interpreter=mi C:\\Users\\
Danpe\\Desktop\\src\\hello.exe"
    }
}
```

This JSON sets our project's folders and settings for SublimeGDB to work. Before trying out GDB, let's compile our C code first by executing the following code:

```
gcc -g hello.c -o hello.exe
```

This will compile our C code in the debug mode, and the output file will be named `hello.exe`. After compiling, we can open the code and start setting breakpoints by going to the desired line and pressing *F9*.

 An OS X user might want to bind this to a different key or disable the **Expose and Spaces** key bindings in the OS X System Preferences.

After toggling a breakpoint, we'll press *F5* to run our executable using SublimeGDB:

```
FOLDERS          hello.c                    x   hello-world.sublime-project  x   hello-world.sublime-workspace  x
  src
    hello.c      1  #include <stdio.h>
                 2
                 3  int main(void)
                 4  {
              •  5      printf("Hello World!\n");
              ›  6      return 0;
                 7  }

                 GDB Session  x   GDB Console  x   GDB Variables  x   GDB Callstack          x     GDB Threads    x   GDB Breakpoints  x
                 1                                              › 1   main();                 1   :op\src\hello.c:5
                                                                  2                            2

  GDB
INSERT MODE, Line 7, Column 2                                                                        Tab Size: 4              C++
```

In the preceding screenshot, we can see our breakpoint on line 5. After pressing *F11* to **Step Into**, we are currently on line 6. At the bottom, we can see the current variables, callstack, threads, and more.

The following table shows a quick summary of all the required shortcuts for debugging with SublimeGDB:

SublimeGDB command	Windows/Linux	OS X
Launch	F5	F5
Exit	Ctrl + F5	Control + F5
Add/remove Breakpoint	F9	F9
Step Over	F10	F10
Step Into	F11	F11
Step Out	Shift + F11	Shift + F11
Continue	F5	F5

Summary

By the end of this chapter, we know how to debug our PHP, JavaScript, and C/C++ code using the best debugging plugins that Sublime's community offers.

We have some homework before the next chapter. We need to think on what's missing in our Sublime Environment. Is there a feature that we are missing? Can we make our coding more productive by adding functionalities to Sublime? After answering one of these questions, we can start the next chapter that will guide us through developing our own plugin for Sublime Text 3!

8
Developing Your Own Plugin

This chapter takes you step-by-step through the process of developing a plugin for Sublime Text and publishing it to the community. In this chapter we will cover the following topics:

- Warming up before starting a plugin
- Starting a plugin
- Developing the plugin
- Publishing our plugin

Warming up before starting a plugin

We have seen that plugins can be very helpful in many situations, so it's time for us to develop our own! Before starting, we need to know a few things; the first is an idea for a plugin. In our case, we will develop a **Ruby on Rails** plugin that will help us identify relationships between **ActiveRecord** models. ActiveRecord models can define relationships with other ActiveRecord models that are defined across different files, creating a plugin that will automatically open all the related files. This plugin can be very helpful for a Rails developer.

It is also important to have the Sublime Text API open simultaneously. It can be found at `http://www.sublimetext.com/docs/3/api_reference.html`. Lets not forget a name for our plugin! In our case, we will call the plugin **RelationsFinder**. The `Default Packages` folder is full of useful open source plugins with code snippets and examples.

Starting a plugin

Sublime can generate a plugin template for us. To generate a plugin, navigate to **Tools | New Plugin...**. Then we should see a screen similar to that shown in the following screenshot:

```
import sublime, sublime_plugin

class ExampleCommand(sublime_plugin.TextCommand):
    def run(self, edit):
        self.view.insert(edit, 0, "Hello, World!")

```

The previous screenshot is what a **"Hello, World!"** plugin looks like. Before starting to write our own code, let's test the following code by saving the file by pressing *Ctrl + S* on Windows or Linux and *Command + S* on OS X. The **Save** dialog will open in the `Packages/User` folder. We don't have to save the file there. We will browse one folder up and create a new folder named `RelationsFinder`. Now let's save the file as `RelationsFinder.py`. The filename doesn't really matter, but the convention is that the file name should be the same as the plugin name. After we've saved the plugin, let's try running it. To run the file, we'll need to open the console by pressing *Ctrl + `* on Windows or Linux and *Control + `* on OS X. Enter the following line in the console to test your new plugin:

```
view.run_command('example')
```

Pressing *Enter* will insert **Hello World!** where the cursor is positioned in our currently open file. Let's try it again, but this time, we'll change the command name from `ExampleCommand` to `RelationsFinderCommand`, as shown in the following screenshot:

```
RelationsFinder.py        x
1    import sublime, sublime_plugin
2
3    class RelationsFinderCommand(sublime_plugin.TextCommand):
4        def run(self, edit):
5            self.view.insert(edit, 0, "Hello, World!")
6

Writing file /C/Users/Danpe/AppData/Roaming/Sublime Text 3/Packages/
reloading plugin RelationsFinder.RelationsFinder


view.run_command('relations_finder')
INSERT MODE, Line 1, Column 1                              Tab Size: 4         Python
```

As you can see in the preceding screenshot, `'relations_finder'` will run `RelationsFinderCommand`. This is Sublime's naming convention for commands. Sublime also provides three different types of commands:

- **Text Command**: This command provides us access to the content of the current file/text via a `View` object.

- **Window Command**: This command provides us access to the current window via a `Window` object

- **Application Command**: This command does not provide access to any specific window/file and is not used commonly. However, this code will run when the application starts.

Since we will be opening views with this plugin, we will use the `sublime_plugin.WindowCommand` class as the base of our command. To do that, we will change our class definition to the following:

```
class RelationsFinderCommand(sublime_plugin.WindowCommand):
```

Then remove the `edit` parameter from our `run` function:

```
def run(self):
    pass
```

Now we want our plugin command to show up in the command palette. Let's create a new file named `RelationsFinder.sublime-commands` and save it in the same folder with the following content:

```
[
    {
        "caption": "RelationsFinder: Find Relations",
        "command": "relations_finder"
    }
]
```

This file will determine which commands we want to expose to the command palette. We will expose our `relations_finder` command by choosing the option `RelationsFinder: Find Relations`. We can now open the command palette by pressing *Ctrl + Shift + P* in Windows or Linux and *Command + Shift + P* in OS X and look for the **RelationsFinder: Find Relations** command, as shown in the following screenshot:

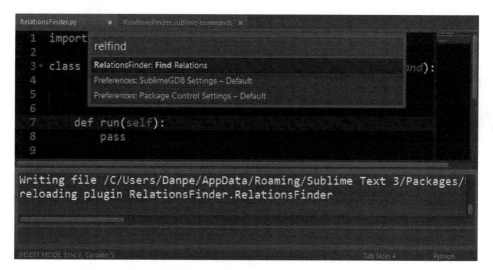

Clicking on the **RelationsFinder: Find Relations** command will execute our `run` command, which currently does nothing.

Developing the plugin

Now that we have a plugin with a basic command that shows up in the command palette, we can start developing our plugin; we'll start with hiding the command when it's unusable. We'll do it by overriding the is_visible function and checking that the current file extension is .rb and the first line contains a ActiveRecord::Base inheritance. Let's import the python os lib by adding import os below the import sublime line. Add the following to our command:

```
def is_visible(self):
    view = self.window.active_view()
    file_name, file_extension = os.path.splitext(view.file_name())
    return file_extension == ".rb" and "ActiveRecord::Base" in view.
substr(view.line(0))
```

When the command palette is being opened, it will run all the is_visible functions of all the exposed commands to check whether or not they should be shown. We are checking whether or not the current view (file) extension is set as .rb and the first line of the file contains ActiveRecord::Base and only if both conditions are true, will this command be visible.

Now we want to scan our file for all the relations. We will use the find_all function of view that retrieves a pattern and returns an array of Regions containing the found pattern. A Region consists of two indexes—a start index and an end index—that together define a string:

```
view = self.window.active_view()
regions = view.find_all("(belongs_to|has_many) :\w+")
```

We will now need to extract the actual string from these regions. We will do it with the substr function of view:

```
for region in regions:
    line = view.substr(region)
```

We might have a problem when a relationship with the user model is written as has_many :users and the filename is user.rb by Rails convention. We will need to clean this string and have a user.rb string:

```
if line.endswith('s'):
    line = line[:-1]
model = line[line.index(":") + 1:] + ".rb"
```

First s is removed and then we cut everything that is after :, adding .rb at the end. The model variable should now hold user.rb. Now, we just need to look for that file in the current project and open it. We will use Python's os.walk to open the file:

```
def open_file_in_project(self, file):
    root = self.window.folders()[0]
    for root, subFolders, files in os.walk(root):
        if file in files:
            self.window.open_file(os.path.join(root, file))
```

The preceding function will scan all folders until it finds the required file and open it using the open_file command of the Window class. The following is the final code:

```
import sublime, sublime_plugin
import os

class RelationsFinderCommand(sublime_plugin.WindowCommand):
    def is_visible(self):
        view = self.window.active_view()
        file-name, file_extension = os.path.splitext(view.file_name())
        return file_extension == ".rb" and "ActiveRecord::Base" in view.substr(view.line(0))

    def run(self):
        view = self.window.active_view()
        regions = view.find_all("(belongs_to|has_many) :\w+")
        for region in regions:
            line = view.substr(region)
            if line.endswith('s'):
                line = line[:-1]
            model = line[line.index(":") + 1:] + ".rb"
            self.open_file_in_project(model)

    def open_file_in_project(self, file):
        root = self.window.folders()[0]
        for root, subFolders, files in os.walk(root):
            if file in files:
                self.window.open_file(os.path.join(root, file))
```

We have covered every line so far; now it's time to test the plugin! Open the model in a **Ruby on Rails** project and call our plugin using the command palette. All relationships instantly open!

 This plugin can be enhanced in a lot of ways, for example, by adding key bindings and supporting has_many_through and :class_name; feel free to improve it.

Publishing our plugin

We are going to publish our plugin to Package Control, so everyone can download and install it. To publish our plugin, we'll need to have `git` installed on our system and a GitHub account. Let's first start by creating a repository for our plugin and committing all files to it by running the following commands in the plugin folder:

```
git init
git add .
git commit -m "Initial Commit"
```

Create a new public repository in GitHub by going to `http://github.com/new` and pushing our local repository there by running:

```
git remote add origin https://github.com/USERNAME/REPO-NAME.git
git push -u origin master
```

In the preceding code, USERNAME is your username and REPO-NAME is the repository name you just created. GitHub will prompt you for the username and password.

> You can also add a README.md file to your repository.

Now for the tricky part: we'll need to select **Fork** on the `https://github.com/wbond/package_control_channel` page, as shown in the following screenshot:

After forking, we'll need to find the right file for adding our plugin to. `package_control_channel/blob/master/repository/X.json`, where X is the first letter of our plugin name. We'll edit this file and add the following code:

```
{
  "name": "RelationsFinder",
  "details": "https://github.com/USERNAME/REPO-NAME",
  "releases": [
    {
      "sublime_text": "*",
      "details": "https://github.com/USERNAME/REPO-NAME/tree/master"
    }
  ]
}
```

Once you're done with editing, click on **Commit Changes** at the bottom of the page:

Now, let's create a pull request for our changes by going back to our forked repository page and clicking on the pull request button, as shown in the following screenshot:

Now all we have left to do is wait for an approval.

 For complete instructions please visit `https://sublime.wbond.net/docs/developers`

Summary

By the end of this chapter, we have developed a simple plugin and published it for the public so that everyone can install it using Package Control!

It is important to know that plugins can have a lot more complicated features and that the Sublime API reference is full of useful functions that help us develop awesome plugins.

That's it; you are now Master of Sublime Text! We would love to see your plugins on the Web.

Index

K

key bindings
  about 42
  advanced key bindings 47
  key map file structure 46
  maintaining 45
  managing 48
  overriding 45
  platform-specific key bindings 46
key map
  about 46
  bindable keys 47
  elements 46
  file structure 46

L

linters
  C/C++ 31
  CoffeeScript 31
  CSS 31
  Haml 31
  HTML 31
  Java 31
  JavaScript 31
  Lua 31
  Objective-J 31
  Perl 31
  PHP 31
  Puppet 31
  Python 31
  Ruby 31
  XML 31
linting 31
load-save mode, SublimeLinter 31
Lua linter 31

M

macros
  about 41
  editing 42
  playing 42
  recording 41
  saved macro, binding 42
  saving 42

Minimalist GNU for Windows (MinGW) 79
Mini Map 14
movement commands, Vintage Mode 60
Multiple Selections 25

O

Objective-J linter 31
on demand mode, SublimeLinter 32

P

Package Control
  installing 18, 19
Package Control snippets
  using 41
Packages directory
  about 12
  user package 13
Perl linter 31
PHP linter 31
PHPUnit
  about 64
  snippets 66
  using 64-66
plugin development
  about 83
  plugin, developing 87, 88
  plugin, publishing 89, 90
  plugin, starting 84-86
projects
  about 27
  build systems 29
  folders 28
  settings 28
  switching 29
Puppet linter 31
Python linter 31
PyUnit 66

R

Regular Expressions 22
RelationsFinder 83
Ruby on Rails plugin 83
RubyTest
  about 69
  bundler autodetect 71

Thank you for buying
Mastering Sublime Text

About Packt Publishing

Packt, pronounced 'packed', published its first book "*Mastering phpMyAdmin for Effective MySQL Management*" in April 2004 and subsequently continued to specialize in publishing highly focused books on specific technologies and solutions.

Our books and publications share the experiences of your fellow IT professionals in adapting and customizing today's systems, applications, and frameworks. Our solution based books give you the knowledge and power to customize the software and technologies you're using to get the job done. Packt books are more specific and less general than the IT books you have seen in the past. Our unique business model allows us to bring you more focused information, giving you more of what you need to know, and less of what you don't.

Packt is a modern, yet unique publishing company, which focuses on producing quality, cutting-edge books for communities of developers, administrators, and newbies alike. For more information, please visit our website: www.packtpub.com.

Writing for Packt

We welcome all inquiries from people who are interested in authoring. Book proposals should be sent to author@packtpub.com. If your book idea is still at an early stage and you would like to discuss it first before writing a formal book proposal, contact us; one of our commissioning editors will get in touch with you.

We're not just looking for published authors; if you have strong technical skills but no writing experience, our experienced editors can help you develop a writing career, or simply get some additional reward for your expertise.

Python 2.6 Text Processing: Beginner's Guide

ISBN: 978-1-84951-212-1   Paperback: 380 pages

The easiest way to learn how to manipulate text with Python

1. The easiest way to learn text processing with Python

2. Deals with the most important textual data formats you will encounter

3. Learn to use the most popular text processing libraries available for Python

4. Packed with examples to guide you through

Mastering TypoScript: TYPO3 Website, Template, and Extension Development

ISBN: 978-1-90481-197-8   Paperback: 400 pages

A complete guide to understanding and using TypoScript, TYPO3's powerful configuration language

1. Powerful control and customization using TypoScript

2. Covers templates, extensions, admin, interface, menus, and database control

3. You don't need to be an experienced PHP developer to use the power of TypoScript

Please check **www.PacktPub.com** for information on our titles

Printed by Amazon Italia Logistica S.r.l.
Torrazza Piemonte (TO), Italy

14958826R00064